INSUFFICIENT POSTAGE
A WEEK IN THE LIFE OF A NEW LETTER CARRIER

KEVIN "KAJEMAN" JOHNSON

Insufficient Postage

Copyright © 2020 by Kevin Johnson

All rights reserved

Published by Red Penguin Books

Bellerose Village, New York

Library of Congress Control Number: 2020924591

ISBN

Print 978-1-63777-381-9

Digital 978-1-63777-382-6

No part of this book may be reproduced in any form or by any electronic or mechanical means, including information storage and retrieval systems, without written permission from the author, except for the use of brief quotations in a book review.

*Mary Johnson who always put her children first.
Marlene Coelho for her assistance,
Amor de minha vida*

FOREWORD

I have come to praise the United States Postal Service, not to bury it.

We all use, rely, depend and even complain about the United States Postal Service, USPS. Yet there is so much about this government agency that we don't know and even take for granted. Did you know that the Postmaster general is the second highest paid government employee after the president. Yes, the Postmaster General gets paid more than the Vice President. The USPS is a highly efficient well oiled machine that delivers over 150 billion pieces of mail annually. That represents 40 percent of all the mail in the world. It is one of the most economical postal systems whereas a a stamp in Europe or Asia is 50 percent more or double than the 55 cents we currently pay. Also the USPS is the only postal service that delivers to every residence in its domain.

The Post Office employs over 520,000 people in various capacities. The most visible and one that we are most familiar with are the Letter Carriers. You probably know who your mailman is. You might chitchat with him, you quite possibly know his name, his days off, and even what time time you think he is supposed to deliver your mail. Your letter carrier gets to know about you. We know if you are behind on bills from late payment notices. We watch your kids grow up and see birthday cards come. When handling your mail we notice the types of magazines you read and from the return address of letters insignificant tidbits of information about you. Unemployment checks, letters from lawyers, acceptance letters from universities, wedding RSVP's heck we can tell who your cable tv contract is with or if you have changed car insurance. Yes we can tell what's going on inside the home from the mail you receive.

There are other various duties that go on some behind the scenes. There are the clerks at the counter. Before self adhesive stamps they were referred to as stamp lickers. They sell you stamps and weigh the packages that you mail. Then you have the other behind the scenes employees such as bulk mailers, truck drivers, janitors and postal police. Let's not forget management. For every six workers there is one individual in management. They mostly just get in the way and keep and worry about ridiculous statistics. Way too many times they feel the need to justify their position and introduce new policies, which do not work. Then we just go back doing our job the right way.

Not too many people grow up aspiring to be a postal worker. You don't hear too often, "I want to be a postal worker" The post office is a job that comes

along and most employees feel they will work there until their dream job presents itself. A more meaningful existence if you will. Either you do get out or the job sucks you in and you get stuck in the rut of a halfway decent paycheck and a six day work week. Before you know it the years fly by and it becomes hard to change and you start counting the years to retirement. There are a number of people who have escaped and moved on to what they were meant to do. Perhaps you've heard of Walt Disney or Charles Lindbergh. Presidents Abraham Lincoln and Harry S Truman worked in the post office. Actor Rock Hudson and even Denzel Washington was a temp. I am sure they are glad that they didn't get stuck in the postal rut.

Again I am not here to put down one of the greatest postal systems unless I want to absolve myself from the truth and lie, "The check is in the mail"

CONTENTS

1. Day One: The Agony of Da Feet	1
2. A Career Choice?	13
3. Hitting the Road Jack with Mick	37
4. Day 2: Like Walking on a Cloud	49
5. I'm a Mailman	63
6. Living Large	73
7. Day 3: All by Myself	81
8. I Meet My Dream Girl	95
9. Day 4: No Hump Day	105
10. Thank God it's...No Big Deal. It's Friday	127
11. Oh, it's Saturday, it's Saturday	147
12. Saturday Night's Alright for...	167
13. Sunday. They Have Mail on Sundays?	177
14. 168 Hours = One Week	185
About the Author	187

DAY ONE: THE AGONY OF DA FEET

I know that I'm in the right place. I can see guys getting out of their cars in a postal letter carrier uniform. I am six minutes away from embarking on my career as a mailman, and I have a bad feeling. I park my car and I'm walking to the Post Office. First day on the job and I must admit that I am nervous. I did not sleep well last night and I'm a tad anxious about this new phase in my life. It was an unusually warm, humid day on June 6th, six minutes before 6:00, and I have a bad, uneasy feeling—an omen, perhaps? It had nothing to do with the 3 sixes—6th day of the sixth month, 6:00 a.m.—666 being the sign of the Devil and all that. The problem was that my feet hurt, and hurt badly.

I was moments away from starting my career as a mailman, and I wore the wrong type of shoe. In the orientation I went to last week, I was instructed to wear black shoes and was told not to wear sneakers. I mean, they insisted that I could not wear sneakers, and the only pair of black shoes that I owned were dress shoes that had a bit of a heel. I walked through the door and as I looked around, I noticed that there were several guys wearing sneakers, some that were not even black. That was my very first experience that the rules were a mere guideline and it was more important to do what was practical and what was in my best interests. I was nervous and uncomfortable, it is *sooo* humid that I was already sweating and my feet hurt. I walked up to the punch clock and there were a bunch of guys, obviously mailmen as they were wearing the uniform. Since it was the summer, most wore shorts but a couple of the guys were wearing long pants. The guys were joking and noticed me right away. I would find out later that new guys stick out like a sore thumb. They asked me if I was a new PTF, although I think they already knew. When I told them yes, they directed me to the letter carrier supervisor's desk.

I noticed there was a short, and when I say short I mean short, really little guy sitting at a desk. Not a midget or dwarf or anything but a really short man. As I approached the desk, the little guy appeared to be mad or at the very least annoyed. Perhaps he was really busy; but from across the room, you could tell that this was not a happy person at the present moment. I stood by the desk and saw that this man's feet did not touch the floor from the seat (like a little kid in a grown-up chair), and I swear that he was so mad that steam seemed to be coming from his head. I was hesitant to bother this little angry man who appeared busy, staring at some papers on his desk. He must have sensed my presence and barked at me without even turning his head: "Are you the new PTF?" Startled, I said, "Y-y-yes, yes I am."

He jumped out of his chair and asked, "Johnson or Hartman? You are obviously not Rodriguez."

I replied, "Johnson."

Then asked, "Do you know where Hartman and Rodriguez are?" I was trying to comprehend the situation. Here was one of the shortest guys I'd ever met and I mean small, maybe around five feet tall. Why was this guy asking me who these people were? I was stunned at how small and angry this guy was. I am only 5'9" and I towered over this little man, thinking this must be what 7-foot guys must feel like all the time. The best way to describe this guy is that he's like a Danny DeVito type. Wrinkled shirt and a vest, shirt sleeves rolled up, tie loosened, balding, obnoxious, disheveled, and not very pleasant to be around. One of the shortest guys I've ever seen. Also, it's not even 6:00 a.m. and this guy was way too angry. His blood pressure must be sky-high. The little man, through brown teeth and a pungent coffee breath odor, asked me again, "Although we get paid by the hour, I do not have time to screw around. Do you know where Hartman and Rodriguez are?" Seriously, this guy hadn't even introduced himself yet and he was way too mad.

So I quickly replied, "I don't know them." More people had gathered by the punch clock, and it seemed they were observing us, laughing and pointing in our direction. The little guy yelled, "Can I see Hartman and Rodriguez?"

Somebody replied, "Not here yet, boss."

So Mr. Stanley Stegman finally introduced himself to me and started ranting, "I am Stanley Stegman, Letter Carrier Supervisor. This is their first day on the job and you would think these guys would be on time. I'm telling you, postal workers used to be more diligent. Not only would they come in on time, they would report ten minutes early to get a feel for the day. They cared about the public that they served." I made the mistake of mentioning that it wasn't 6:00 a.m. yet. Mr. Stegman gave me a look. I suddenly realized this was a topic that I should not have commented on. "Let me tell you, back in the day, postal workers had respect for authority. They did not, I repeat, did not talk back to their supervisor. They had too much respect to…" Stanley Stegman looked past me in mid-sentence. "Okay, Rodriguez is here." I turned towards the punch clock and the crowd was bigger. A couple of guys in uniform were talking to a tall Spanish-looking guy in jeans. It seemed kind of racist to me at first that Mr. Stegman assumed this guy was Rodriguez. Later on, I figured out that after some time on this mundane job, it was a lot like the movie *Ground Hog Day* where every day's the same. So it was easy to notice when anything was out of the ordinary.

The guys were talking to whom we assumed was Rodriguez.

They pointed at Stegman and the guy started walking towards us. Stegman mumbled something. I think I heard him say, "Big ass Cro-Magnon man."

The man quickly approached us and said, "Hi there, my name is Manny Rodriguez and I am looking for a Mr. Stanley Stegman"

"I am Stegman. Also, I am the Carrier Supervisor. I don't know why you would be confused as to which one of us is the man in charge."

"No confusion, I just don't want to make any mistakes on my first day," replied Rodriguez.

"Oh, you're gonna make mistakes today and many in the future."

"Well, I will try to minimize my mistakes. It is my pleasure to meet you; I am at your service, Mr. Stegman."

Stegman replied sarcastically "Ha, at my service. You can just call me Stan or Mr. Stegman will do. By the way, how tall are you, Rodriguez?"

"I'm 6'5 inches tall and my friends call me Roddy."

Stegman sternly said, "I am not your friend. Both of you listen to me. What I need is I need you to do your job, come in every day on time, and do not cause me any problem. Do you understand?"

I replied, "Yes," and my fellow PTF Rodriguez said, "Of course, I will."

"Okay then, follow me to the PM's office. I'm not waiting for Hartman." Stegman turned and started walking away; and for a little guy, he could move. Those little legs could move, just churning away. I had to hurry to keep up, but Roddy didn't seem to have to exert as much energy with his long 6'5" strides.

I thought Stegman was sizing up Roddy for his uniform and that I should let him know how tall I was, so I mentioned to Stegman, "Hey Stan, I am 5'9".

He looked at me bewildered and said, "What?"

So I repeated, "I'm 5'9"."

He seemed even more confused. "So what? Are you trying to rub it in? You're taller than me, congratulations."

I replied, "Oh, no. I thought you needed to know our heights for our uniforms."

"Uniforms? Uniforms? You're not getting uniforms for three more months, if you are lucky and don't piss me off. Remember, you're a PTF—Part-Time Flexible. You'll be on probation for 90 days."

As we followed Stegman, we passed a bunch of guys sitting in chairs flicking letters into cubby holes. Some were really fast, others not doing much of anything. There were about eight people there, three women and five guys. Three of the guys started saying things like: "Look at the newbies. Don't hurt them, Steggy. Which one do you think will make it?" It was literally like a prison movie.

We finally got to an office marked "PostMaster." Ah, Post Master. That's what Stegman meant when he said the PM's office. I was not about to ask him, and to be perfectly honest, I ran through my mind all of the PMs I was familiar with: Prime minister or AM-PM. We went into the office and it was very plain. An American Flag stood in the corner, and there was a desk and a couple of chairs. A television was in one corner on a pushcart and what looked like a DVD player hooked up to it. A couple of chairs were lined up against the wall, and two chairs were in front of the desk. Stegman hopped in the chair behind the desk but did not indicate for us to sit down. My feet were aching and I would not mind sitting, but the gaffe I made about mentioning my height to Stegman was fresh in my mind. I was nervous and Stegman appeared to get pissed off easily. Stegman looked at us and said, "I'm required to say 'Welcome to the United States Post Office,' and some other horse crap, so welcome. Let's get it straight. You were hired as PTFs, part-time flexible employees, but you will probably be working at least 50 hours a week. As a matter of fact, I need somebody to work this Sunday, real easy—two hours and you get time and a quarter.

You pick up outgoing letters from the busy mailboxes in downtown Farmingburg, go to Regional to get express mail, and deliver them, if possible. So, any volunteers?" Stegman looked directly at me, and to appease him I quickly said, "I'm available."

Stegman replied, "I didn't ask if you are available. I asked if you would do it. I'm taking that as a yes. I need you to answer the questions that I ask. I do not have all day to repeat myself. I have a lot to do here, we are one of the busiest Post Offices on Long Island. Our numbers here are outstanding, our productivity is up, and we need dedicated, hard workers here. If you wanted a Country Club Post Office, you should have gone to Bethpage. They are ranked dead last in the Long Island Regional Productivity Report, 42nd out of 42. Their Letter Carrier Supervisor should be fired. We are Number 2 on Long Island and are striving for Number 1. We are going to knock Melville out from the top spot. It just so happens that their Letter Carrier Supervisor is the Regional Director's son. That's the Regional Director's picture on the wall, Reginald Wellington." I noticed some pictures on the wall and assumed that it was a chain of command as the last two pictures were the PostMaster General and the President of the United States… I noticed Roddy smiling and shaking his head up and down in agreement, seemingly interested in everything Stegman was saying.

My pea brain was spinning, my feet hurt, I wish I could sit down, and I wish I went to the Bethpage Post Office if it was a Country Club. I lived in Bethpage for eight years. As a kid, I remember my mailman, Mr. Ray. He was always happy, giving us rubber bands from his truck. Sometimes we would sell lemonade and Mr. Ray would buy some and overpay. Damn, I wish I went to Bethpage…

Then Stegman went off on a tangent. "I single-handedly brought this Post Office out of mediocrity. We went from 18th to 2nd, Number 2 on the RPR. Anybody could keep Melville Number 1, that's why P.J. Wellington is Letter Carrier Supervisor there. It's nepotism; he's the Director's son. He's not there on merit. I deserved Melville." Then Stegman's rant took a weird, dark turn: "I'll tell you why. They are discriminating against me because of my height. That's right, I'm 5 foot 1. That's what it says on my driver's license. Are you aware there has never been a U.S. President less than 5 foot 4?" In the modern-day era, not one shorter than 5 foot 10.

So I was thinking, *5 foot 1? I think he's exaggerating. He looks shorter and, like me, he's wearing shoes with heels.* Speaking of shoes, I'm buying a black pair of comfortable shoes as soon as I get out of here, probably Skechers.

But this guy's got major issues, comparing himself to United States Presidents."You see, I am the Number 1 Supervisor on Long Island. Nobody, nobody should have gotten that slot but me. Melville is the Mecca, right near Regional Headquarters. I would be around the hotshot big wigs. They would not be able to overlook my administrative skills. Boom, right up the executive ladder, get my mother off my back. It's a curse having a Jewish mother and successful siblings. My brother Jeffrey, a lawyer, my other brother Ira, a doctor. When she's with her friends she goes on and on about them. I get 20 seconds: 'Stanley? He's still in the Post Office.' The lowly civil servant, killing himself slowly, giving it his all, not being recognized for his accomplishments. If I'd get the promotions I deserve, maybe once, just once, I'd get top billing over my brothers. And my wife doesn't help either. She dated Jeffrey before me. 'Go back to school,' she nags. 'Go back to school, it's not too late. You can do something with your life.' I am doing something! If I was only a couple of inches taller. You tall guys get all the breaks, opportunities up the ying-yang, sports, forget about it. Do you know I'm a really good basketball player? I can dribble all around you, Rodriguez. I can shoot from outside and pass. I am a wizard."

Rodriguez replied, "Oh, I don't play basketball. Mr. Stegman. I play football which you call soccer."

Stegman ignored him and continued, "Any guy seven-foot tall should be good. Shaquille O'Neal? Come on, 50% from the free-throw line. Now, you take Spud Webb and Muggsy Bogues. They were basketball players, five foot nothing and playing in the NBA. That's an athlete. I think Dr. Naismith would have made the basket higher than 10 feet if he knew these Neanderthals would be reaching up and slamming it down too easy, way too easy. It bothers me so much when tall guys don't have heart and motivation and are not grateful. Okay, Johnson. So you're 5'9" and you are working Sunday."

I'd completely forgot about Sunday. So much weird stuff had happened in my 45-minute postal career. I was tired, my feet hurt, and my head was spinning. Roddy chimed in, "Mr. Stegman, I am so happy to be here. I will work hard and diligently and say a prayer that you get the promotion that you deserve." This was when it dawned on me that Roddy was a first-class kiss ass. I don't know why it took me so long to figure that out. And if so, why was I working Sunday? Kiss ass should be working instead of me.

Stegman tells us to follow him, and we once again walk past the clerks. As if they were caged animals, our mere presence got them wound up and excited. Another brief encounter with this group, but this time I was not chasing Stegman into the PM's office. I was able to get a better look at the group that taunted us 10 minutes prior and, oh boy, wow. For the most part, they were not an attractive bunch. One guy was dressed in green pants and an orange polka dot shirt. Who dressed this guy? One guy must have been 6 foot 6 inches. Stegman must be really jealous of this guy. Another guy was average height. For argument's sake, let's say 5 foot 9. Suddenly, I was conscious of people's heights. It seems that I inherited Stegman's insecurities, but he was heavy, well over three hundred pounds and hairy—long hair and a beard. There was a lady with way too much make-up on who waved sheepishly to Roddy. Of course, he smiled and waved back.

Then they started. The fat guy said, "Hey Gordon, they were in there a long time. What did ol' Stegman tell them?"

"I'm sure they got the short version of how he's gonna be the PostMaster General someday."

Fat guy said, "Yeah, the short version."

Stegman glared at the fat guy. "I gave them a wide spectrum of postal info, Mr. Flacco, a very wide spectrum."

Mr. Flacco replied, "So you're going with Fat Jokes, Steggy? Going with the obvious? Best you can do?"

Stegman just moved quickly past this motley crew. Again, I just tried to keep up with him. "Don't mind the savages. Their bark is worse than their bite. You'll get used to it."

I was thinking, *I've got to get used to this?*

As we approached the Carrier Supervisor's desk, with Stegman still moving quickly, he observed, "Hey, look, Hartman is here!" Again, I thought, *How does he know this?* There was a young guy sitting in the chair that I first saw Stegman sitting in. The guy was sitting there looking somewhat amused, swiveling in Stegman's chair. Stegman asked, "Has there been a coup? Last that I checked, that was my chair."

Hartman stopped spinning and said, "Yo, yo, the guys told me to wait here, yo. I figured that I would take a load off the old dogs cause we gonna be walking all day, yo."

Stegman seemed more amused than annoyed, "Please, we speak the King's English in this office. Get out of my chair, Mr. Hartman; and you were late and missed my orientation. Do you offer any explanation?"

Hartman stood up and said, "Yo no, no yo, no, my bad, yo."

Stegman, again more amused than mad, replied, "Yes, you are bad. You are late, you are sitting in my chair, and this is your first day. Let's see what else is in store for us. This is going to be amusing, to say the least. Alright, gentlemen, let's go punch-in. Come with me."

My first reaction was, *Punch-in now?* We have been here for over half an hour, my feet can tell you that. I was thinking, *We should get paid for the time we have been here,* although I wasn't going to bring that up now. I had to admit I was intimidated by Stegman's temper.

Hartman informed us, "Yo, the guys made me punch-in when I got here. They showed me my card and somebody showed me how to do it, yo, and told me to wait for you, which I did."

Stegman's amusement for Hartman turned to outward annoyance. The tone of his voice turned to disgust as he spit out, "You were late AND you missed my orientation. Let's get this straight, you were hired to work for Farmingburg Post Office as a PTF letter carrier. I am the Carrier Supervisor. I am responsible for everything associated with delivering mail in Farmingburg, understood? I am the Grand Poobah here, the Big Cheese, El Cap-i-tain, *Jefe* for my *amigo*, Roddy. You screw up, I go down with the ship. Your actions reflect how I am doing my job. I know your type, Hartman. You are privileged and don't even know it. Oh, your ship is gonna come in one day, but you will be at the airport."

Hartman retorted, "I've never been on a plane, yo. How 'bout we deliver some mail, yo."

Stegman answered, "Roddy, I'm liking you so much more in the last five minutes. Maybe we can be friends, *compadres* if you will, before I commit myself. So gentleman, the punch-in the card, with your respective names. We will be going digital, maybe even thumb readers. For the time being, we are doing it the old fashioned way."

I was thinking, *We've been here almost an hour.*

"The Post Office breaks down an hour, sixty minutes, into 100 units. You are allowed to be eight units late to punch-in, approximately five minutes before you are officially late. Mr. Hartman, you were more than eight units late today. I am not going to hold that against you today. I'm sure I will have plenty of time to write you up in the near future. Remember, you are on a 90-day probationary period, lateness will not be tolerated." As

Stegman was talking to us, a letter carrier by the punch clock was throwing mail into his route case. But as he flicked each letter, he was kind of funny to watch. I was mesmerized by this man's movements. He kind of lurched forward every time he threw a letter.

Stegman interrupted the silence, "Okay, yo, Mr. Hartman. You go with George here. Johnson, you are going with McSwanson, and Roddy, my friend, you will be going with Bobby Lamore. So I followed Stegman over to route 26 to meet McSwanson.

A CAREER CHOICE?

I was still amazed at how fast Stegman moved. I finally caught up to him, and he introduced me to McSwanson. I'm guessing that he was a couple of years older than me. He says hello, turns around with his back to me, and starts sorting letters. "So you want to be a mailman!?" I was looking at route 26. It appeared that all the routes were the same—L shaped. In front, the letter card consisted of five horizontal shelves with a light on top. Each shelf had 30 cubbyholes going across it so that each address was identified by the number underneath the name of the address. Each street name was listed and written larger to the left, and perpendicular to the letter case was the flat case. Flats were magazines, newspapers, junk mail, and letters that were larger than standardized letters, with the cases acting as a wall barrier. Each route was right next to each other, so the next guy's flat case was like a wall for your route. It was similar to a 12 square foot cubicle with six-foot walls. For anyone to approach, they would have to come in the back opening. It was cozy as it was somewhat private. If you were facing the letter case, you were in your own little world. There were a couple of trays of letters and a couple more trays of junk mail. McSwanson had a handful of letters in his hand and he was sorting the letters fast. He asked again, "So you want to be a mailman?"

I told him, "Well, I am currently out of work and I need a job. I desperately need cash."

"Yeah, money makes the world go around, but what else have you done? What did you want to be? What were your dreams?"

I replied, "Well, I just got out of the military. I was in the Army, and I was an Electronic Technician. I put in an application with the town. They have openings with the Sewer Department, troubleshooting switches and gauges. I saw that the Long Island Rail Road has jobs in that field, and then this came along. I took the postal test before I went into the Army and they passed me over, so they put me back on the list and they called. Voila, here I am."

McSwanson responded, "All I'm saying is you didn't grow up saying I want to be a mailman. This is where dreams die. You start working here, it's a six-day workweek. You very rarely get two days off in a row. The pay is not so bad in the beginning; but as a carrier, it's a dead-end job. There's overtime every day if you want it. It's a rut, paycheck to paycheck, paying for cars and rent, or worse, a mortgage. It sucks you in, and as time goes by it's harder to do what you want to do in life or, more importantly, what you were meant to do in this lifetime." He stopped throwing letters and turned to me, looked me straight in the eyes, and solemnly said, "My advice? Do not get stuck in the rut! It's a bitch to get out of." I thought to myself, *Wow, I'm here about an hour and a half. I'm taking it minute by minute, let alone day by day and this guy was talking about getting stuck in a rut, mortgages, car payments? I'm living with my parents.* My head was spinning.

McSwanson said, "Come on, I'll show you the kickback case." He informed me that most of the mail we get in our trays were for our route, but there were mistakes so we kick them back. The clerks then re-sort them and hopefully, the mail gets to the right route. The clerks were the people over by the PM's office.

My mind went back to the encounter with the clerks. "Oh yeah, there was a really tall guy."

"Yeah, that's Gordon, tall and skinny; and I'm sure Robard stood out with his clothes. He's an artist. You know how I told you this job kills dreams? Well, Robard is a tad eccentric. You would think he gets dressed in the dark. He chooses to dress that way. He's not a mental case. I don't know if it's because he wants attention or he just does not care. He is interesting to observe. He is an artist—he paints. The dude can't match an outfit; but damn, that guy is an awesome artist. His paintings are small, like a credit card or a matchbox. So much detail. I'm not an art critic, but he should get his stuff evaluated."

We got to the kickback case; it was about 4 and 1/2 feet tall. McSwanson showed me where the kickback letters went, and there was a place for kickback flats and other cubbyholes for Moved, Left No Forwarding Address (MLNA), Forwarding Order Expired (FOE), and others I didn't understand.

McSwanson explained, "This is where you will see the 'hat dance.' It's pretty funny. Also, behind here is the parcel section. You check that last before you leave the office for the street." Behind the kickback case was another series of shelves. Here, the clerks sorted parcels by route, a wall about 4 feet high, another U-shaped area where you can see packages sorted out.

There was a container of parcels, and the lady clerk with too much make-up was taking the packages one by one to each specific route. She saw us and waved to McSwanson, "Hey Mick, I see you got a new guy."

McSwanson replied, "Yeah. Good morning, Suzy. This is Kevin Johnson. He obviously started today."

"Pleased to meet you, Mr. Johnson. You're lucky to be with Mick. He is one of the best. We, well I, love him."

McSwanson responded, "Wait for it."

She continued, "It's going to be hazy, hot, and humid—triple

H's—so it's important to drink lots of water and wear loose clothing."

I replied, "Okay, thanks, Suzy."

She went on, "And don't forget the sunblock, even if it's cloudy." She continued to sort packages, and we turned to go back to route 26. Mick informed me that the carriers called her Suzy Forecast. She would always tell us what the weather was going to be and offer advice. It wasn't her job or anything, it's just what she does.

I saw the floor layout of Farmingburg Post Office a lot clearer now, and one side. "You had the L-shaped route cases. They were lined up next to each other and, if not against a wall of the building, they were back to back. The cases formed aisles in between the kickback case. The parcel section was in the middle, and the clerks were on the other side along with the offices. Stegman's desk was placed strategically at the front. From his desk, he could look into the opening of the route cases and observe if the carrier was working or even there. Guys would leave their route cubicle to go to the bathroom, kickbacks, smoke, or even goof off.

We walked past Stegman, who looked annoyed, and McSwanson said, "Hey Stanley, Johnson here is a keeper, I bet he makes it."

Stegman snorted," That's wonderful, you made my day."

I was following McSwanson and noticed that he moved quickly, too. It was like these people were possessed to get where they were going. He turned to me. I was three strides behind and he said, "You will get used to the pace."

I told him that my shoes were bothering me.

Mick looked down. "Oh, yeah. You should not have worn those shoes."

There were two guys heading our way, they both had on uniforms. One guy was tall and the other was short. The short guy said, "Hey Pitt, we're getting a whole bunch of new guys today. Hey Mick, how are you doing?"

McSwanson responded, "Hey Yates, good. Yeah, this guy is following me today. This is Johnson."

"'J,' this is Pittman and Yates." The little guy, Yates, nodded and smiled at me.

The taller guy, Pittman, said to me, "Well, good luck. Whatever Mick tells you to do, do the opposite."

Yates mentioned to McSwanson, "Hey, we're playing at the Modern Times bar on Saturday night. We'll be looking for you in the audience."

McSwanson answered, "You know, if I'm not busy, I'm there."

Yates extended the invitation, "J, You can come, too."

I thanked him. McSwanson turned and walked away and Pittman and Yates went their way. I noticed no parting words, I mean, they didn't shake my hand. They were nice, but everybody seemed to be in a hurry here. McSwanson explained to me that they were in a speed metal band called Morbid Obesity. He said they were really good. I also noticed as we headed back to route 26 that the routes were not in chronological order, 1, 2, 3, but randomly, 15, 45, 23.

At route 29, a guy was standing there throwing flats. He had red hair and a red face. He saw MacSwanson and said, "You Irish bastard, maybe we go out today and have that drink."

Mick replied, "Ah, you know I'm on the wagon. Hey, this is one of the new guys, Johnson, I call him 'J.' This is Jimmy McGregor."

Macgregor's face grew redder. "First off, do not listen to this ignoramus. My name is Jimmy (real fast) MacGregor, not McGregor. Got it? MacGregor."

I replied, "MacGregor, yes sir. MacGregor."

"I'm telling you, do not listen to the lush. His brain is so screwed up with all the drinking." I looked over at McSwanson and he was not only not offended, he was laughing. He turned into route 26, so I followed him. As I walked away, I heard MacGregor say, "As long as I'm alive I will never understand the

Irish." McSwanson explained that he loved to get MacGregor all tight by screwing with his name and anything that would make his face red.

My feet were in pain and I think McSwanson sensed it because he told me to have a seat. Every route had a stool that was stored underneath the case. I gladly sat down, a little slice of heaven, as I had been standing for over two hours so far; and we hadn't even started to walk the route yet. McSwanson informed me that we would not be driving in a jeep but would be walking out of the office pushing one of those three-wheeled carts. I was somewhat disappointed because I wanted to drive a postal jeep, especially a right-sided steering wheeled vehicle. Normal cars have the steering wheels on the left-hand side, whereas the Post Office jeep had the steering wheels on the right-hand side. So if it was curbed delivery, the letter carrier just had to stick his arm out of the vehicle and put the mail in the box. Plus, my feet hurt and it would have been nice to sit down. McSwanson told me to look at the flat case, that every time I do a new route I should familiarize myself with the streets that are on that particular route. He pointed out that the numbers would go up and then down. These were called loops. In residential areas, you might have noticed the letter carrier pull up and park. The letter carrier then starts walking on one side of the street to the end of the block. On the case, this would correspond to the numbers on the particular street, let's say, 20, 22, 24, 26, 28, 32. The letter carrier would then cross the street to 31, 27, 25, 23, and 21. So the case goes down in that sequence. The next loop would start at 34, 36, 38, to 48, up even, then down 47, 45 to 33, odd. It was very confusing at first but got easier as you did it more. Like a computer keyboard, some people were highly proficient, able to type really fast without even looking. Others, like me, were two fingers hunt and peck. So I was studying the flat case and enjoying not having to stand, being able to sit on the stool. I guess, to the casual observer, it might appear that I was not doing much of anything.

McSwanson let me know that break time was soon and that happened whenever the coffee truck pulled up outside and blew his horn. I'm thinking, *Cool, break time, more time for me to rest my feet.* So I was sitting on the stool at the end of the flat case and all of a sudden Stegman was standing next to me. I turned my head and we were face to face, literally eye to eye, less than a foot apart.

Stegman asked me, "You comfortable, Johnson?"

I was startled, thinking, *Where did this guy come from? I've only been sitting down for a minute, maybe two.* I stammered, "I, I, I'm studying the flat case."

McSwanson chimed in, "Yeah boss, I told him to have a seat and study the flat case. His feet are sore. Look at the shoes he wore."

Stegman looked down, "Holy crap, what were you thinking?"

I replied, "They told me not to wear sneakers, and these were the only black shoes that I had."

He answered, "I hope you make it through the day. I suggest you get a comfortable pair of shoes toot sweet, ASAP, yesterday." Stegman turned to McSwanson, "I need you to rack an hour on route 16. Peterson called in sick again. Johnson, you are going solo for a while here throwing letters. Please, don't spend too much time studying, it's not a test."

Before I knew it, they both were gone. So I picked up a handful of mail. Man, this was so much harder than it looked. When I observed other guys, the mail was moving fast out of their hands and into the letter case. I was to find out later that you could get written up if you did not throw at least 18 letters a minute. 18 letters a minute. Seems like a lot, but you actually had to throw a lot faster than that. I was probably doing six a minute. All of a sudden, a guy showed up looking for Mick. I let him know that McSwanson was on route 16. The guy, in a heavy Brooklyn Italian accent, introduced himself as Joey Rigolleto,

"The guys call me Joey Rags." He then looked down at my shoes and said, "Those shoes don't look comfortable."

I replied that they were not comfortable at all. I wonder how he knew about my shoes. He then mentioned that he was a Union representative and wanted to welcome me to the NALC. The Union was the National Association of Letter Carriers, the NALC. Each craft within the Post Office, the clerks, letter carriers, truck deliverers, all had different Unions. Even the PostMasters were in the PostMaster Association. Joey Rags then asked me what I was doing prior to working there, and I told him that I was discharged from the Army.

Joey made a sound, "Pffff, I was a Marine." He then asked me where Hartman was. Apparently, at orientation when they had us fill out our W2's, we filled out paperwork allowing the Union to automatically take our dues out of our paychecks. Hartman did not fill out this form and Joey Rags wanted, no needed, to rectify this situation. At the orientation, they informed us that the Union could not represent us during our 90-day probation, and Hartman must have thought, *So what am I paying dues for?* It dawned on me that I should have waited 90 days, too. Joey informed me that there was a Union meeting during the break that was going to be held in the break room. He told me to get new shoes and then quickly departed. Less than two minutes went by and I heard a horn. Somebody shouted out, "Take a break."

Roddy came up to me and asked how I was doing. I told him that I was casing letters. He told me that he was sorting flats and then asked me if I met Joey Rags, the Assistant Shop Steward. I said that I did but did not mention that he was the assistant.

Roddy asked me "What's with your shoes? People are talking about them."

I replied, "My shoes are Army dress shoes and they're very uncomfortable."

"You need to get comfortable shoes my friend, very important."

I responded, "Nobody knows right now how important comfortable shoes are, nobody!"

Hartman came over. "Yo, yo, yo, can I borrow $10? I forgot my wallet and I want to get something from the coffee truck. Aren't you guys hungry?" I was thinking, *I'm nervous, tired, and my feet are killing me. Hungry? I mean, sure I'll eat something.*

"Alright my friends, I'm buying this morning. Let's go," declared Roddy.

I was feeling pretty good about my new acquaintance and accepted his offer. As we went outside, some of the other carriers had already bought their breakfast and were heading back in. It seemed like there were groups or cliques of guys. Some said hello, and some were asking, "Who is 'Shoes?'"

Hartman asked, "Yo, 'Who is Shoes?' Yo?"

Roddy pointed down and Hartman remarked, "Yo, your day is gonna suck, yo."

"My day sucks already."

Hartman replied, "Yo, you need a different pair of shoes, yo."

I'm like, "Yeah, yeah, gotta get comfy shoes." At the coffee truck, I got chocolate milk and a buttered bagel. My man Roddy got coffee and an apple. Hartman got an egg sandwich, two sodas, a Danish, and a bag of potato chips. My boy was not shy about helping himself. Our new friend Roddy paid, like he said he would. It seemed we were last at the coffee truck, and the coffee truck guy winked at us and said, "Good luck, new guys," as he closed up and prepared to leave.

Hartman nodded and said, "Yo, word up."

I thanked Roddy and he asked, "How did he know we were new?"

I said, "Well, we were last, we look like we're lost, he has never seen us before, and we were not wearing uniforms."

Hartman, drinking his soda, burped out loud, "Yo, we stand out like a sore thumb, yo."

Roddy asked him, "Can you ever say anything without saying, 'Yo, yo?'"

Hartman just said, "Yes."

As we returned to the office, it was like a ghost town. All the cases were empty, and Stegman was down the middle aisle of cases looking annoyed.

Flacco was at the kickback case collecting letters and flats. He seemed different than when we first encountered him. He seemed friendly and not hostile like before. It was as if he was out of his element over here in the carrier section. He asked us, "How's it going, guys?" He looked down at our feet and then looked up at me. Here it comes, "Dude, you have to get new shoes."

I say, "Thanks. Where is everybody?" Flacco told us that if nobody was around they were probably in the break room. I remembered Joey Rags telling us about the Union meeting. So we headed over to the break room which was in the corner of the office, next to the bathroom across from the clerk section. The three of us went into the break room; and it was packed with 50 or so letter carriers, all in uniform. Some were wearing Post Office t-shirts or sweatshirts instead of the uniform shirt. There were two huge tables pushed together with about 20 guys sitting in chairs around the table. My first reaction was of being pissed off because I wanted to sit down and rest my feet, but we stood against the wall like the other 30 guys who didn't get to sit down. At the head of the table was Joey Rags and another guy. He was about 6 foot 2, in shape, broad shoulders, square jaw, crew cut drill sergeant type.

We found out this guy was David Letterman, our Union Representative. He was talking about the M.41 and the upcoming contract negotiations. We didn't understand anything this guy was talking about. I found out later the M.41 is the Carrier Handbook. Joey Rags saw us and motioned to Letterman. Letterman kept talking about the M.41, for a couple of minutes. He then acknowledged us. "Okay, guys, we have 3 new PTF's. Make them feel welcome. Help them out like you were helped out when you first started. Welcome guys. If you can stick around after, I will fill you in some more on Union biz." I noticed that some of the guys were looking over at us. Some smiled or nodded, some were looking down at my feet and were snickering and laughing. I hoped they all got a good laugh at my expense.

Letterman then announced, "We have one last bit of news. Our very own Dimitri Del Greco is being honored today by the newspapers and the mayor for alerting the residents of a home on Lockwood Drive that their house was on fire. One of the residents was an elderly grandmother who could have been caught in the fire upstairs in her room. Letter carrier Del Greco rushed in as the house was about to go up in flames and assisted the residents and the family pets to safety. "A round of applause for Del Greco."

A loud roar filled the room, guys clapping saying, "Good job, Grec," "Atta boy." But a couple of guys chanted Mona, Mona, Mona. I had no clue why they were chanting Mona. Letterman closed the meeting by saying, "Safety first guys, safety first, and remember, 'The walls have ears.'"

So much had happened since I walked through the door, and there had been so much to absorb and all this weird strange terminology. I didn't know what they were talking about because everything was so fast-paced. There was no time to stop and ask questions about everything that was so foreign to me. The meeting was apparently over because guys were walking out the door of the break room. Some of the guys stopped to shake our hands and say welcome. One guy introduced himself as Pierre Seavall and in a French accent advised us, "Get out now. Don't do it. Get out!!!!"

Another guy who said his name was Chooch and told us, "Aw, it's not that bad. It is what it is."

The room cleared out except for me and my new associates,

Roddy, Hartman, Joey Rags, and Letterman. Letterman called us over and asked, "Who is Hartman?"

Hartman just says, "Yo."

Letterman told him, "We have, well let me correct myself, we had 100% participation in the Union."

Joey Rays repeated, "Yeah, we had 100%."

Hartman informed them, "Yo, I was told you couldn't, like, represent me for the first 90 days, yo, so I figured it was like a waste of money, right?"

Letterman got indignant, "The NALC, a waste of money?" like it was the dumbest thing that he had ever heard.

"Yo, no, not your Union. I'm talking 'bout my money, yo. I don't have much and I have three kids and another one on the way."

Roddy and I turned to each other in amazement—three kids and one more in the oven? First off, this guy was barely 20 years old. His behavior, as I could evaluate after knowing him for two hours, would be totally irresponsible. I hope he was more conscientious when raising his kids.

Letterman explained, "Well, it is true that we cannot officially represent you, but there is a lot that we can do for you."

Joey Rags added, "Yeah, behind the scenes, if you know what I mean." All three of us nodded yes, although none of us knew what he meant.

Letterman continued, "Do whatever management asks of you. Basically, do your job; but remember if you are here to stay, you have to stand up for yourself. If you leave the office an hour late, you come back an hour later than normal, don't run routes, you make the guy who has to do the route every day, day after day, rain or shine, look bad."

Joey Rags repeated, "Yeah, don't run routes and make us guys look bad. Pfff, if I leave the office an hour late, I come back an hour and a half later."

Letterman advised, "I don't suggest that; but if there is anything we can do, let us know. Any questions?"

"Hello, I'm Manny Rodriguez. You can call me Roddy. It's a pleasure to meet both of you guys. I am proud to be part of the Union; but you said the walls have ears, what does that mean?"

Letterman explained, "Watch what you say around the office. We get casual and talk about things that might give management information. The Post Office is very top-heavy, one person in management for every worker, and their main job is to make their numbers look good at your expense so they can move up and get promoted. Most Supervisors were letter carriers or clerks. They usually could not do the job or do it well. Supervisors get promoted to their level of incompetence. Also, there are catacombs, little spaces that the Postal Police and Inspectors use to watch us so that they can catch postal employees doing inappropriate things, like dealing drugs or stealing. The sanctity of the mail and the public trust of our customers is critical. Johnny, our custodian, tips us off when they have him clean out the cobwebs and wash the one-way windows. That is usually an indicator they are coming. When we leave here, you can see around the perimeter of the floor there are mirrors up top. They are one-way windows where Inspectors can spy on us without us being able to see them. Just like in a relationship, if you don't trust your spouse what kind of relationship do you have? So no opening mail, no reading magazines, and absolutely, absolutely, do not steal anything. If you obey these simple rules, you won't have any problems; but every now and then, you get individuals who think they are slick and slick themselves right out of a career in the USPS."

I couldn't help but think, *Not only do the walls have ears, they have eyes and handcuffs.* I've always heard that opening someone else's mail was a Federal offense. I didn't know exactly what that meant, but you're not going to catch me opening mail, stealing, or reading magazines. I wanted to keep this job until I got on my feet.

Hartman asked, "Yo, so if I leave an hour later than usual, what does that mean, like, paycheck wise, yo?"

Joey Rags chimed in, "An hour overtime at time and a half."

"Cha-Ching, yo. I can use the extra moolah, yo."

Letterman wrapped up, "Okay, guys, time to get back to work. Break time should be just about over. You don't want Supervisor Stegman mad at you on your first day. He is actually a very hard worker and used to be a letter carrier in another office."

I mentioned that he already seemed mad at us as we were walking out of the break room.

Joey Rags explained, "Stegman is alright. You give him a fair shake and he won't bust your balls. He has a lot to deal with, but the dude has issues. I mean, to go with the obvious, he has a major Napoleon complex."

Roddy said, "He also told us about his successful brothers."

"Pfff, he told you about Jeffrey and Ira?? Hahaha." We were walking by the clerk section and they overheard us, so Gordo and Flacco went into a routine.

Gordo said, "So, Mrs. Stegman, how is your son Ira?"

Flacco answered in a high-pitched voice pretending to be Stegman's mother, "My son Ira is doing well. He is a very successful lawyer, you know."

Gordo replied, "And how is your son Jeffrey?"

Flacco responded again in the same high-pitched voice, "Jeffrey is a doctor and he is considering running for public office."

Gordo continued, "And how is little Stanley?"

Flacco's voice became stern and lost its high pitch, "I don't have a son Stanley!"

Everybody laughed as we continued walking back to the carrier side. As we passed the parcel section, Stegman came out of nowhere. He was apparently very stealthy, able to sneak up on you quickly without you being able to notice.

"Alright ladies, break time is over. Routes 10 to 32 final sweep." So I walked back to route 26 which was in the middle aisle and got the flat cart. Every route had a flat cart, a four-wheeled canvas pull cart about 2 feet deep, 4 feet long, and 2 feet wide. I started to pull the cart, but nobody in the middle aisle was doing that

Chooch saw me and said, "Hey Shoes, we are not 10 through 32, that's the first aisle. It starts at route 10 and ends at 32. Although you are on route 26, we don't go yet. We are 23 through 37. It is what it is."

I got it. The first route in the U-shaped aisle was route 23 and went around to 37. Okay, I went back to racking mail, wondering how I was going to shake my nickname 'Shoes." I didn't like it. I didn't want to be 'Shoes.'

Two or three minutes later McSwanson came back. "Hey J, you know you guys already have nicknames."

I replied, "Yeah, yeah, I'm Shoes. What's Roddy?"

"I don't know but the kid is Yo-yo. Let's do a final sweep."

Just at that moment, Stegman yelled, "5 through 17… sweep." As we were walking over to the clerk section, guys from the first aisle were coming back with their carts full. Stegman was standing there with a clipboard writing something as each carrier walked past. McSwanson noticed that I was looking and informed me that Stegman was counting the mail. Mail was counted in length, not by the piece which would be absurd, but by how many feet there was. Each tray was two feet; and as each carrier walked past Stegman, he estimated how much mail by the foot each route had just gotten.

McSwanson told me all the mail that we cased was counted, and that went into the reports and compared to other offices on Long Island. It was how Regional kept tabs on productivity. It seemed like a lot of effort for mere statistics. As we went around the clerk section, clerks and carriers bantered back and forth, small talk and verbal jabs. We collected flats for our route, and as we went by Flacco, I could swear he was sleeping. McSwanson told me he worked another full-time job and caught a couple of winks of sleep here and there. We headed back to the carrier section and Stegman counted our mail. As we walked down the aisle, McSwanson introduced me to some of the 'guys' which was actually incorrect as there were female carriers also. "Hey Steve-o, Gravy Train, this here is J, one of the new guys that started today." The carrier at 17 stopped what he was doing and turned around.

He said to me, "Hey, Steve Graves here. Nice to meet you." He picked up some flats and started throwing them as he stood sideways to talk. "What did you do before this?" he asked.

I explained that I was recently discharged from the Army, Fort Bliss, Texas. He informed me he was Air Force. He proceeded to tell me to have a nice day. He then added, "And do yourself a favor and get some different shoes." I didn't respond. Didn't anybody realize that I knew that I wore the wrong shoes?

"Next up," Mick said, "the Bruce." Mick rolled his R's when he said Bruce. "So J, this here is the Bruce; the Bruce, this here is J." The Bruce just looked up and waved and we moved to the next route. A cute redhead turned around, smiled at me, and said, "Hi, I'm Maybel." I then realized that I had been staring at her extremely large breasts. When I finally looked up, I realized that I was busted, and Maybel smiled even more. "Cat got your tongue, J? Well, good luck and have a nice day."

Mick teased me "J, you are embarrassing me. You know you're blushing." We got to the next guy, "This is one of my favorite guys in the world. Catfish, Catfish Tommy Moore. Catfish is from down south, Georgia as a matter of fact."

Catfish was an older black gentleman; and he said in a slow, deliberate way with a southern drawl, "Remember that today is your only first day in the Post Office, I hope you enjoy it. You sure got a good teacher."

"Thank you, sir," I replied as we moved on to the next route.

"Over here we have Steve Mueller. Steve is a bit of an enigma, an introvert, a loner."

Steve turned around. He looked a bit menacing. "No disrespect, Mick, but last names are not important. And no disrespect to you, new guy, but you don't need to know my business and I certainly don't want to know anything about your business, *Capeesh?*"

We proceeded to the next route, route 7 and Mick announced, "And in this corner weighing in at a buck sixty is our very own, Syd Weir."

Syd stopped what he was doing, pointed at me, and said, "Nice to meet you, welcome aboard."

Mick told me that Syd was an MMA fighter on a two-fight win streak. Syd walked past us and pointed to the kickback case. "Kickbacks" was all he said.

As Mick walked, he asked me, "Do you gamble, J? Because this is our rambling gambling man, Chooch. Lots of the guys here have a system. Whatever team Chooch is going for, they bet on the other team."

Chooch responded, "It is what it is. Hey, Mick. Hey, Shoes. Yeah, I'm liking the Yankees tonight. C.C.'s on the mound."

Mick reminded me, "Go the other way, works more often than it doesn't."

Chooch responded, " I'm telling you, I like my Yanks. It is what it is."

The next route was an older gentleman, Dittmeyer. Mick introduced me, "Hey, Ditt. This is J, one of the new guys."

Dittmeyer said, "Wonderful, I've got two working days left. All I can say is good luck." He turned around real quick. Mick mentioned that Dittmeyer was retiring in two days and he might bid on his route. When a carrier leaves a route, that route is put up for bid. The most senior carrier that bids on the route gets it.

Yates walked past and said," Hey, Mick. I wanted Ditt's route when he's gone."

Dittmeyer retorted, "What do you mean, 'When I'm gone?' I'm not dying, I'm just moving to Florida, a slow death." To tell the truth, Ditt did look worn out.

At the end of the routes, there was a way to slip through to the next set of routes. Mick told me that this group of routes was the business section. Farmingburg had quite a few factories, warehouses, and retail stores. Mick informed me that the business routes typically had more mail volume, but they didn't have to hump a mailbag all day long although some of the routes were part business and part residential. The first carrier we saw was Dotty Parker. Dotty was attractive. She was in good shape—a soccer mom. Mick explained that Dotty played in two softball leagues and was a really good player. Dotty didn't even turn around. She just said hello.

At the next route, Benjy Steckle was having a conversation with Joey Rags. "Hey, Joe, have you spoken with the PM about providing us with sunscreen and bug repellant? I would hate to get melanoma or West Nile if it could be avoided, and I don't think we should have to buy it ourselves. It is an occupational hazard, after all."

Joey Rags responded, "Pfff, me and Letterman are meeting with the PM today. I should have an answer for you later."

Benjy replied, "Thanks, Joe. Hey, Mick, you walking the new guy?"

Mick responded, "Yup, this is J."

Benjy said, "Hi."

The next two routes were two young guys who were wearing knit ski hats. They both had longish hair and were wearing black t-shirts and uniform pants. Mick told me that these were the ski boys. I asked, "Are they called that because they ski a lot?"

Mick responded, "No, it's because they're Polish." The first guy was tall and skinny and Mick introduced me to Joey Ramonski.

Joey just blurted out, "Almost done here. What up, new guy?"

The individual next to him was going somewhere and he stopped. Mick introduced me, "This is Chris, 'Where's Your House Key,' Wojohowski."

Chris told me, "You can call me Chris or Wojo."

I informed him that he could call me Kevin or J.

Chris said, "Or I can call you Shoes." God, I hate that. Chris turned to Mick and asked, "You going to the Morbid Obesity show Saturday night? The guys are in great form. They're really shredding it. There is going to be music people there. You know, agents and label people."

Mick responded that he should be there. Mick noticed Stegman going around asking how late each route was going to be. Mick went back the way we came through the back routes so we didn't have to encounter Stegman. As we headed back to Mick's route, he told me the Ski Boys were the setup guys, or the roadies, if you will, for Pittman and Yates's band, Morbid Obesity. We were back at the route and Mick instructed, "Try to finish the letters. I'll be pulling down the flats. Then the accountable cart will come by."

I inquired, "What's on the accountable cart?"

Mick explained, "Certified, insured, and registered mail, plus we have to sign for our keys to the relay boxes."

"Alright. I understand certified and registered mail, but what are the relay boxes?"

"Have you ever seen the green mailboxes?" Mick asked.

"I have, but they're closed. You can't open them and put mail in."

"Exactly," Mick said. "We are going to put relays, sorted mail, into these plastic bins and they are going to be dropped off in one of those green boxes. When we finish a relay, we will have delivered all the mail we were carrying. There will be a green relay box. We will open it and get the mail for the next relay. There are five green boxes on our route that coincide with the next series of deliveries. We can't carry all the mail for the route with us in our cart, so it's broken into relays. Luckily, we have the timid one dropping off our relays. He will get them there on time. There are two drop off guys; they are the parcel post guys —PP1 and PP2. Timmy is PP2. PP1 is a guy named Floyd Lloyd, a real jerk. He's connected, not to the mob or anything, but his mother and sister are some kind of hotshots, Regional Manager or ex-PostMasters, something like that. This guy doesn't care about anything. I'm not as gung ho as the Union rep, but I give a crap about the people on my route and the reputation of the Post Office; and I care about my fellow carriers, too."

As he said this, Joey Ramoneski walked by and said, "Yo, Mick is telling the new guy that he loves us."

As if on cue, I heard a buzz among the carrier section. I turned to see a big cart moving into our area. I heard the guys calling out a catcall.

"Loose Lucy, watcha doing tonight?"

"Oughta be, who you doin' tonight?"

I heard a voice, sweet and angelic, say, "Guys, if you are lucky it might be you."

I turned to see what the commotion was about. They say quality of life was not how many breaths you take, rather it was how many moments that take your breath away. This was a moment that I will always remember. Now, I must advise you that I have an obsession with Spanish girls. I love them, *me gusta Latinas*. The olive skin, the long or short dark hair, the way they walk, the way they dress, nice tight pants, and the way they show their cleavage. For me, they ooze sexiness. I turned to see a goddess, Lucy Consuelo Gonzales-Nieves Martinez Smith, for the very first time and my jaw dropped and my heart sputtered. It was love, well lust actually, lust at first sight. If I could have created a woman from scratch, the end product would be Lucy. Long black hair, full lips, nice butt, tight pants, high heels, great tits, at least D cups, with plenty of cleavage showing. I just stared. She noticed me looking and smiled. I melted.

"I see we have some new guys", she said.

Mick snapped me out of my trance, "You like that, J? Let me tell you, she is so cool."

"Cool? That is the most beautiful woman I have ever seen!!" All of a sudden, my feet didn't hurt anymore. Lucy started calling guys over to her cart. They went over and signed for accountable mail and keys to mailboxes. She would banter with the guys. You could hear a lot of laughing. Mick told me she liked to joke with them and make sexual innuendos.

I thought, *OMG, she looks this hot and she is a guy's girl.* Mick told me that she occasionally comes to the bar after work and hangs out with the guys; and she likes to talk, well, joke about sex. She doesn't drive so guys give her a ride home and a couple of guys claimed to have had her. So I started making plans to hang out at the bar quite often. Mick told me she has one child, a boy named Julien, about six years old. She was divorced from a guy named Smith which was where she got her last name, but she wouldn't change it so that she had the same name as her son. So I was gathering up her background info and she got to Del Greco.

Lucy said, "Hey, it's our big hero. Congratulations!"

Greco replied, "Lucy, I'm thinking if *con* in Spanish means with, like *arroz con pollo* means rice with chicken, does Consuelo mean with swallow?" You know con with, and suelo swallow?"

"Del Greco, you talk dirty too much and don't back it up. I know you are a mona."

"That's right, Lucy. I do moan a lot."

"No, Del Greco. Mona—M.O.N.A.—Man of No Action. If I begged you to drive me home right now, you would come up lame."

"I love you, Lucy, but it's somebody else's turn to drive. Let me sign for this so I can go to the bathroom and do a selfie. God, you got me all worked up!"

"Greco, you need a woman and maybe you'll stop jerking off."

"I get mine, Lucy, I get mine. If you need a ride home tonight, I'm your guy." I could barely believe what I was hearing. After seeing this gorgeous creature and talking about masturbation, I was ready to go to the bathroom and rub one out, too.

Lucy turned to me and Mick. "Okay, route 26. Come get your accountables."

Mick said, "Hey, Lucy. We don't want too many certified. It slows me down."

Lucy replied, "None today, just your keys."

She turned to me. "Hello, you must be *Choose*. You need to get a more comfortable pair of shoes."

I stammered, "Yes, they told me not to wear sneakers and these were the only black pair that I had".

"Poor baby. Your feet must hurt."

Again, I melted. "Yes, a little." I'm trying to be macho. Mick was back at the route pulling down the sorted mail and Lucy moved on to the next route.

"You appear to be smitten, my friend". Mick observed.

"I'm head over heels, buddy boy," I replied.

Mick said, "Let's get out on the road. I would have shown you how to write up accountables, but we didn't have any. When we do get certified mail, they are mostly from banks or motor vehicle. At the apartments, I just leave the little yellow notice. I don't knock on the door. I will if I know they're home; but mostly, I leave notice or I lose out on my free time. You have to cut corners to make up time."

McSwanson was putting the flats (magazine size) and sorted letters, rubber-banded up in those white plastic boxes, and labeling them for the relay boxes. He was also throwing in small parcels, like a box of checks, in the corresponding white box. Our parcel post guy, Tim Watts, was pushing a skid with other walk-out routes.

He said to McSwanson, "There are three large parcels. I'll deliver them, Mick."

"Thanks, Tim. U Da Man."

Tim replied, "No, U Da Man."

I looked around and about half the routes were pulling down and the other half was still sorting mail. I asked Mick, "So if they leave late, they come back late, right?" We were at least an hour late.

Stegman walked by almost like he was waiting and listening

and said, "New guys back on time. McSwanson, if you're still delivering mail, cut him loose and send him back so he can get used to punching out on time."

"You got it, Stan the man," Mick answered him.

It was kind of strange when people were talking about you when you're standing right next to them. I turned around and Lucy and my man Roddy were in some conversation in Spanish. Lucy was laughing and I was somewhat jealous. She said, "Hey guys, this new guy might take me off the market. He is *sooo* cute. Look at his butt, Mamacita likes."

Now I was really jealous, but Mick got me out of my moment. He'd already pulled everything out of the case and put it in the three-wheeled cart. "Our chariot awaits, my friend. Let's go to the bathroom, tap our kidneys, and wash our hands. Mail is dirty, you will be surprised. Probably as dirty as money, paper bills. Of course, we don't realize it."

So we walked to the bathroom and I realized half the guys were gone. I noticed that the case was empty. When I first walked in this morning, there was mail everywhere, trays of letters, magazines, flats, junk mail. Now every route was devoid of all mail, and the chair (stool) was put underneath the ledge. The clerk section was empty of the clerks. I asked Mick where they went and he said they were probably at lunch and that once we were gone, the energy level of the office goes way down. The only busy part was the counter where they sell stamps and deal with customers.

As we walked into the bathroom, I was overcome by the stench. Mick said Flacco is or was here. "Breathe through your mouth," Mick advised. "I have Febreeze triple strength. It says it eliminates odors. There is no, and I mean no, spray that can get rid of that smell."

Flacco emerged from a bathroom stall and seemed proud of his ability to stink out a whole bathroom. Another gem, gentleman, another gem. I took care of business and washed my hands. They were a lot dirtier than I thought.

Mick was washing his hands and said, "Told you so. Mail is dirty and try not to touch your face or rub your eyes when casing mail. Bad things, man, bad things."

We walked back to route 26 and again more carriers were gone or pulling down. We grabbed our pushcart and headed to the clock because we had to punch out when we hit the road.

Mick explained, "It's another way to keep tabs on us."

HITTING THE ROAD JACK WITH MICK

So we left the office and Mick was pushing the cart while I followed next to him. Although the office was air-conditioned, it seemed a tad warm inside; but when we hit the street, you could really feel the heat. After all, it was June and the sun was shining; but it was the humidity that was killing me. Although my feet were in pain, it was different from the standing-in-one-spot kind of pain. Mick was making small talk about life in the Post Office and how nice it was not to be confined inside on a nice day like today.

He informed me, "Don't get me wrong, there are crappy days, real crappy days in a row. Do you know what it is like pushing this cart in the snow? Not easy, they should give me a snowmobile. Some days, ice is easier than snow and slush. If it's a light day, I just carry a shoulder bag. But I could just not imagine sitting in an office every day doing the same old thing day after day. Look at those clerks in our office, if they weren't crazy before, that job made them crazy. I swear, they are all mentally ill. I mean, nice people but I'd rather stick needles in my eyes than to do what they do."

We were walking past a porch where an elderly couple

smiled and waved. "Hello, Mr. and Mrs. Portsmith, beautiful day! George is on his way."

"Hello, Mick," the woman replied, obviously Mrs. Portsmith.

"Why couldn't you be our mailman again instead of that jackass, George?" Mr. Portsmith asked. "We would get our mail so much sooner."

"Aw, that's just the way the route is set up," responded Mick.

Old man Portsmith then asked, "Why does he walk so funny? Maybe if he didn't bop like that we would get our mail sooner!"

"They changed the route, Mr. Portsmith. That's why I changed to this route. Sorry I left, but George is doing the best he can. Maybe you can complain to management, but they are always changing things. They believe it is for the best, whether it is or isn't. Management thinks they know everything." We said goodbye to the Portsmiths and continued our route.

A Post Office jeep passed us and honked. Mick waved to him. "On the corner is our first stop, the Sunnyside Up deli. Do you want free coffee?"

A couple of kids rode by and said hello to Mick. Mick explained that he used to have George, "The Bird's" route, five years ago. He had that route for four years and knew those kids since they were three and now they were twelve. Like the Portsmiths, not only had he gotten to know these people, but he had also gotten to know a lot about them.

"You see lots of interpersonal things happen to the people on your route. Births, death, divorce, loss of jobs, graduations, and more. Sometimes you can find out by the mail. Like all of a sudden, the father is getting an unemployment check. The mail tells you what's going on inside the home."

We arrived at the deli and behind the counter was a gorgeous young Middle Eastern girl. She smiled when she saw Mick. "Hey, Angie, how are you today?" Mick inquired.

"Good, very good, Mick," she replied.

"This is a new guy, I call him J. It's his first day on the job."

Angie smiled at me. "Congratulations, J. Would you like something to drink, coffee maybe?"

Now I don't want to be rude, but who the heck drinks coffee on a 90-degree day? So I said, "No, thank you." I regretted it right away that I didn't ask for a bottle of water or soda. We said goodbye and headed out the door. The next stop was a commercial building with multiple offices.

The first stop was an insurance company and the air-conditioning was cranking. The receptionist was attractive and really happy to see Mick. They made small talk as Mick delivered the mail and Rhonda gave him the outgoing mail. We walked out and went into an accountant's office. We repeated the scenario and again everyone was happy to see Mick. Guys in suits called out, "Hey, Mick!" One offered baseball tickets for the weekend, which Mick accepted. We didn't go into every office, though, which seemed strange.

On the way out, there was a mailbox that Mick opened and placed mail for the offices we didn't go to. Mick explained, "I go into the offices that give me a Christmas tip. If they don't, their mail goes in the outside mailbox. Alright, I might make an exception if they have an incredibly hot receptionist that I wouldn't mind taking out."

A guy came down to the mailbox as we were walking away and he seemed annoyed at us. It appeared that there were two types of mail customers. One that was happy to see us and appreciated the service we performed. Then you have the ones that were critical of us and somewhat resentful.

Thank goodness, Mick's route did not have a lot of walking. Instead, there were quite a few apartment buildings and office buildings. My feet still hurt, but it was better than standing in one place. The pretty receptionists also helped take my mind off my hurting feet. There was a McDonald's coming up, and I realized how thirsty I was. We actually ran out of mail to deliver and approached one of those dull green mailboxes. Mick explained that Tom Watts had already dropped off the white mail tubs full of racked mail. We opened the green box and, as Mick promised, our white tub of mail was there. We loaded our cart and continued on our merry way. We had been walking for about an hour and fifteen minutes and Mick explained that we were making good time and were about one-third of the way done with our route.

We stopped at Mickey D's for lunch and Mick bought me a soda and a dollar menu cheeseburger. I wasn't complaining that soda was *sooo* good. I asked him about the offices that we didn't bring the mail into, that maybe they would complain to management. He told me he never had that problem. The trick was to just say the other company had accountable mail, like certified or registered mail. He said that management always lied to the public. They would tell the public that a guy was already on the street when the carrier hadn't even left the building.

He said, "Forwarding mail? Nobody has time to actually do forwarding. We deliver it and if the new customer gives the mail back, we forward it. Of course, if they're a good tipper then we take the time out to forward the mail."

I was really loving the air-conditioning and sitting down, but Mick said it was time to go. We headed out and; again, after enjoying the air-conditioning inside, it felt hotter outside. We delivered to a couple of apartments and then finally reached the end of the road we were on.

We were about to cross the street, this route was on a busy road, Route 103. It was not a major highway, but it was also not a side street. We crossed to a car repair shop. Again, we went about dropping off the mail and picking up outgoing mail. Next door was a coffee shop, and Mick told me that it was not really a coffee shop but more of a social club for a bunch of older Irish guys. Mick told me that they called themselves the Easties. They moved out to Long Island 30-40 years ago from Brooklyn and the Bronx. They had accents and pronounced 33rd Street as Turdy

Turd Street. Mick told me the boss, Mr. Benedict, actually nailed a guy's hand to a telephone pole 35 years ago because he deserved it. These were tough guys who were past their prime but were still dangerous.

They smiled when they saw Mick. One guy yelled out "Our Mick, the best mailman!"

Mick replied, "Leo, my man."

Leo asked, "Mick, have I told you the story about me at the Copa?"

"Yes, you have, Leo, a couple of times. Hey, this is a new guy. His name is Johnson, but we call him J."

Leo said, "Nice to meet you, J. Stop by any time for a drink. We normally don't like guys in uniform and especially government workers, but we make an exception for postal workers."

"We appreciate that, Leo," said Mick. "We're falling behind. I'll see you tomorrow."

Leo replied, "Yeah, youse guys get on your way."

Mick said that they were a good group of guys, but they do some skeevy stuff that I didn't want to know about. We delivered to a couple of more businesses, stopped at another green box, and picked up more mail. We were almost across the street at the intersection of Route 103 where we had started a couple of hours earlier.

We had one last apartment building left and it was huge. Mick explained that this building alone was an hour's worth of delivering on this route but should take us 20 minutes. We entered the building; and I saw Lamore, the letter carrier, going into the elevator. I asked Mick about it, and he told me that Lamore had lots of girlfriends here in Farmingburg, even though he was married. He'd had to move further east on Long Island so that when he was out with his wife he didn't run into one of the girls he was messing with.

I noticed that there was a wall of mailboxes. Mick told me that there was a room that runs behind the wall of mailboxes. We went through the door, and Mick turned on the light. There was a long aisle where only one guy would be able to stand. We walked all the way to the end and there were rows and rows of boxes about three by five inches. These boxes were labeled at the top to indicate which apartment it was for. Mick faced the back of each mailbox. Because we sorted the mail, it was all in order so Mick put the mail in the boxes—about ten boxes left to right, then down one row, and ten boxes left to right, then down another row, and so on. Once you finished, you moved down to the next set of ten boxes and repeated the process. Mick was moving really fast and was not talking so I just observed. Then it happened. I sensed something moving to my left. I looked and there was a hand that someone was putting all the way through from the front of the mailbox. The hand came through and was turning to try to get, well steal, mail from the other boxes. I nudged Mick and he smacked the hand with the magazines in his hand and yelled, "Beauregard, how many times do I have to tell you not to take other people's mail?"

"Oh, Mick, Mrs. Weber asked me to get her mail for her."

"We both know she would have given you her key or put it on hold."

"Okay, Mick, don't tell her."

Mick went back to delivering the mail to the boxes. As we came out of the room, we saw Lamore going out the front door. Mick said, "That guy is my hero."

He then said, "J, you must be hungry. There's a great pizza joint right across the street. Let's eat, I'm buying. You're going to love this place. By the way, how are your feet feeling?"

"I'm more thirsty than hungry, and my feet are done for the day." I didn't want to whine, but the dogs were killing me. We went into the pizza place, The Leaning Tower o' Pizza, and noticed Steve Mueller sitting at a table all by himself. Steve seemed to be really enjoying his meal and didn't even see us come in. Mick said that Steve ate there a lot but never saw him with anyone else. "That's his prerogative," Mick quipped, "if he wants to sit alone, let him." He continued, "The food here is the best Italian food around. Order anything you like, my man." I ordered a slice and a large soda. I didn't want to be like Yo-yo, taking advantage and ordering too much. Mick ordered a meatball parmigiana hero. We took our seats and Steve looked over at us. Mick and Steve just nodded to each other and Steve looked at me and nodded again. So I nodded in return and he looked down at my shoes and kind of smirked and went back to his meal. As I sat there, my feet felt relieved. It was at this point that I realized that my first day of walking was pretty much done. I made it! Mick and I made small talk. Mostly he gave me advice on how to get by as a letter carrier.

"You do your job and don't piss off Stegman. You will figure out what you can and what you can't get away with. Most importantly, do not, I repeat, do not bring any unwanted attention to yourself."

Our order was ready and Mick was so right, This was a delicious pizza. I finished my soda way too fast and I noticed Mueller leaving without any acknowledgment of us. Mick seemed to be really enjoying his meatball hero as we made small talk. Gravity set in as I enjoyed the comfy confines of this fine establishment, and the time flew by. Mick was done eating and mentioned that it was time to go.

As we went out the door of the Leaning Tower and its air-conditioning, the heat and humidity smacked us right in the face. Mick informed me that I had to go back and punch in and he had to kill an hour for the time he spent racking mail on the other route. So Mick was getting an hour overtime. I understood that it was my first day and I was beyond ready to get out of these shoes.

We walked back to the office and Mick gave me the cart. He told me to put it in front of his case and he would take care of it later. He left and went to the parking lot to get in his car. I was walking past the apartments that we passed earlier that day. I saw Mr. Portsmith sans Mrs. Portsmith and I waved. He came by the fence and I greeted him, "Hey, Mr. Portsmith." He started telling me that it was 2:30 and he still hadn't received his mail. He went on a tirade about the lousy service that the Post Office provided and the ridiculous price of a stamp. He then started cursing out his carrier George and making fun of the way he walked. "He's late because of that stupid hitch in his step." Now I remembered that they called George "The Bird," and I assumed it was because of the way he walked. Also, Yo-yo was walking with George today. "George is a jackass and your esteemed supervisor, Mr. Stegman, is a jackass and your buddy Mick is a jackass for changing routes. To tell you the truth, I think that anyone who works for the Post Office is a jackass!" I knew that I should be offended, but I assumed that if Mrs. Portsmith were here he might not be so opinionated. I was positive she would put him in his place. I told Mr. Portsmith that it was my first day and I hoped that this job was temporary, that I was hoping that the railroad called. Mr Portsmith then started ranting that I should become a supervisor. Because postal supervisors only lie and pass the buck. I looked at my watch and I realized that I really had to go. So I delicately ended our conversation and walked away.

That didn't stop Mr. Portsmith as he kept yelling how much the Post Office did not meet his expectations. Well, that was a delicate way to put it. I was walking pretty quickly towards the office and my feet were reminding me again that I wore the wrong shoes today. See, I did not need anybody else to point it out for me. Suddenly, it dawned on me that I just might see Lucy Consuelo Gonzales-Nieves Martinez Smith, and all of a sudden my feet hurt a little less.

As I walked into the office, I noticed Hartman sitting in the supervisor's chair with his foot up, similar to the first time I laid eyes on him. I called, "Yo, yo, waz up?" Hartman explained that he got pooped on by a bunch of pigeons that a postal customer kept at his house. While running from the skyfall of dung, he slipped on the poop and fell, and hurt his ankle and hip.

Yo-yo said "Yo, I think this guy George can communicate with the birds, yo. There was so much crap falling from the sky, yo. It was everywhere, yo. I've never seen anything like it, yo. And yo, get this, George doesn't, like yo, get any poop on him. Nothing, yo. Like yo, maybe it's like a professional courtesy with the birds or something, yo. And let me tell you, yo, that shit, and I do mean shit, is slippery, yo. Can you see how much my ankle is swollen?"

I had to admit his ankle didn't look all that swollen, but hey, I'm no doctor. Yo-yo told me they were taking him to urgent care to get x-rays. "Can you believe the Post Office is taking me to a storefront doctor? A doctor in a box."

Yo-yo was still carrying on when it happened. I saw Lucy. She was talking to a guy in a shirt and tie. I interrupted Hartman, "Who is the guy talking to Lucy?"

Hartman responded, "Yo, that guy is the night time supervisor, Mike the Mortician. Yo, they got nicknames for everybody, yo. Stegman went home already, yo, and the clerks are mostly gone too, a couple still here." Well, it figured, Stegman was here before us. First in, first out. The carrier section looked so different now. Earlier that day there were people buzzing around and there was mail everywhere. So much energy. Now it was calm and empty, devoid of mail and energy for the most part.

Lucy and this Mortician guy were walking towards us. Lucy was smiling and laughing. I realized that I didn't even know this guy, but I didn't like him at this moment. God, Lucy looked so beautiful and our eyes met. She smiled and waved and said, "Hi, *Choose*."

I responded, "Hey, Lucy."

Mike the Mortician said, "And you must be Rodriguez."

I'm thinking this guy is stupid, too. I blurted out, "No, I'm Johnson."

And he replied, "No, him."

I turned around and Roddy was standing right behind me.

Roddy immediately started sucking up to the Mortician guy. Lucy turned and asked Yo-yo about his ankle. *Hey, I'm thinking, What about me?* I'm sure that I have a couple of blisters on my feet that are way more painful and swollen than this clown's ankle.

Lucy turned to me "Kevin, you made it through your first day with those ridiculous *choose*. It must have been so hard."

Oh my God, she knows my name. She knows my name. I stammered, "It wasn't that bad." That was all I had? I felt so stupid.

Lucy replied, "Oh, they need me at the window" and turned and walked away. I just watched her walk away so elegantly, but so sexily, too.

Mike the Mortician introduced himself to me. I shook his hand and noticed that he was tall, and spoke slowly and deliberately. He had these dark circles around his eyes. Hence the nickname Mortician. Mike informed me that he was the nighttime supervisor and reminded me to get new shoes.

I noticed a crowd forming by the punch clock, and Roddy and I were about to head over there when we noticed a woman walking towards us in a business suit. As she walked up to us, she said, "Excuse me, new PTF's, Johnson and Rodriguez. Hello, I'm Nancy Cummings the Superintendent of Postal Operations."

"Nice to meet you, Ms. Cummings."

She said, "Mike, I need the route reports and then I will cover you as you bring Mr. Hartman here to the urgent care."

Roddy told Cummings, "That's a beautiful business suit that you are wearing. The color is perfect for you."

Cummings appeared appreciative of Roddy's comment and smiled coyly. "Thank you. It's actually a man's suit, but it fits me perfectly." She turned to Mike, "Again, Mike, the reports."

Roddy waved and said, "Goodbye, Ms. Cummings. It truly is my pleasure to be working here at the Farmingburg Post Office."

Cummings was already talking to Yo-yo and, for the most part, ignored Roddy. We walked to the punch-out clock and in the crowd was Dotty, Dittmeyer, Joey Ramonski, and Del Greco. I pointed back and forth at them, "Dit dit dot dit dit dot dot dit dot dot," my military training morse code. Joey Ramonski and Dotty got the joke and laughed. The joke definitely went over Roddy's head.

Roddy turned to Del Greco. "Congratulations on your heroic deed."

Del Greco seemed focused on Nancy Cummings and said, "I just did what anybody else would do, you know, the right thing. I tell you the SPO really fills out that suit. She said it's a man's suit. I wonder which man left it behind. Yeah, I'd do her."

Joey Ramonski winked and said, "You aren't in management, Greco. You know she only does guys in regionals. You know, working on a promotion."

Del Greco chuckled, "Yup, she goes down to move up. You know what I would love, her and Lucy getting together and..."

Suddenly, Roddy interrupted, " Mr. Greco the guys in the breakroom called you MONA. I was wondering what that meant."

Joey Ramonski stepped in and said, "Hey, Grec, the guy doesn't mean anything by it." Dotty and Dittmeyer laughed at Roddy's faux pax.

Del Greco said, "No, I don't care. They say man of no action —MONA. Hey, I'm a sexual being. I like sex, no, I love sex. I'm not like these sexually repressed robots here. They say I'm a man of no action. Well, I'm no Lamore, but I get mine. More than most of you."

There was an awkward pause until Dotty stated, "It's 3 o'clock people. Let's get out of here." Just in time. It was finally 3:00 p.m. and my first day was officially over when we punched out.

Wow, it seemed like such a long time since I walked through the doors this morning. I realized because of the time we spent with Stegman's orientation I wouldn't be getting paid for eight hours. It didn't seem fair as Yo-yo was probably going to get overtime because he would be at the urgent care which he referred to as a doctor in a box. I left the office with Roddy. As we walked across the loading dock, some carriers were backing up to unload. Jeeps were coming down the street and they were not the most cautious drivers I have come across. Some jeeps were going fast, really fast. The office parking lot was maybe a third full. I guess guys were getting overtime. Roddy told me about his day with Lamore. He says that Lamore was a real playboy with quite a few admirers that live on his route. Roddy estimated that he personally did 90% of the route. He said that Lamore would leave him at the beginning of a loop and then take off. He didn't know what Lamore was doing, but he wasn't delivering mail. He assumed that he was visiting his admirers. At lunchtime, Lamore drove to the McDonald's and left him there. Lamore walked across the street to the apartments. I told Roddy that I was at those apartments when Lamore came in and that he left about 25 minutes later when we were done. I then told Roddy about my encounter with Beauregard and we both laughed our asses off. We both commented on the situations we had and how weird some of our peers were. Roddy told me he expected me to have new shoes tomorrow. I told him that I would, and I didn't expect that anybody would be calling me Shoes anymore. We got in our respective cars and drove off. It was then that I took a deep breath. Day one was over, over, over. I proceeded to drive to the mall to buy the most comfortable pair of black sneakers I could find.

DAY 2: LIKE WALKING ON A CLOUD

Man did I sleep well. It was one of the best nights of sleep I ever had. But that alarm clock was awfully rude at 5:20 a.m. I had to be at work at 6:30 so I showered and got dressed. I then proceeded to put on my brand new memory foam sneakers. Ah, a little slice of heaven, like walking on a cloud I tell you. I left my house and drove to the Farmingburg Post Office. As I pulled up around 6:15, I again saw carriers coming to work. I walked across the loading dock and entered the building. I saw carriers hovering by the punch clock and figured that I should utilize the restroom. On my way there, I ran into Letterman. He asked, "How was your first day? You're Johnson, right?"

I told him, "Yes, I'm Johnson, and my first day was interesting to say the least. I bought some new shoes, and I'm looking forward to today."

Letterman informed me that if I was going to make a career of this, my feet needed to be taken care of. He also stated the need to have top of the line bedding and mattress, as we spend one third of our life in bed.

I never thought of it like that and replied, "You can't argue with that logic."

Letterman then informed me that there was a coffee pot in

the breakroom and was invited to help myself, although at the beginning of the month Joey Rags collects $5 for the coffee, milk, and cream from everyone who drinks the coffee. As we were new, they were letting us drink coffee gratis until the end of the month. I thanked Letterman but told him that I don't drink coffee. I mentioned that I would rather have a Diet Coke. Just as I said this, Roddy and Lamore came out of the breakroom; and they were both carrying coffee cups and laughing. Letterman asked Lamore if he contributed to the coffee fund. Lamore told Letterman that he would when he saw Joey.

Letterman retorted, "You say that all the time and never do. It's not fair to the other guys who chip in."

"Alright, Dave. By the way, it's only a half cup," Lamore responded. I observed Roddy and Lamore standing next to each other and noticed that they were very similar. Tall, in good shape, dark complexion, and I guess they could be described as handsome.

I went to the bathroom and then headed to the punch clock. There were 12-15 guys waiting to punch in. I saw McSwanson and he smiled and said, "Hey, J, what's up? Guys, look, J got a new pair of shoes. How are the dogs making out?"

"Oh man, they feel much better. It's like walking on a cloud," I replied.

Right away I noticed some carriers that I definitely did not see yesterday. I noticed this big, no huge, white guy, probably in his thirties with long dreadlocks and a beard. It dawned on me that this was how the guys recognized me yesterday so fast. Anything out of the ordinary stuck out, it was so easy to identify. The big guy looked at me and asked, "What, are you new? How you doin'? I'm Quentin, Quentin Roosevelt." He then held out his hand to shake. Wow, took a whole day before anyone shook my hand here.

I told the big man, "Yes, yesterday was my first day, I'm Kevin Johnson, and I'm pleased to meet you."

"Oh yeah. First day sucks."

I saw Catfish and I'm reminded of what he said yesterday, so I repeated, "Yup, yesterday was the only first day that I was gonna have here."

Catfish heard me and quipped, "And you are only gonna get one second day, too. Enjoy them."

Quentin just said, "Oh yeah."

I heard Chooch explaining how he lost his bet on the Yankees. "C.C. just had an off night, you know. It is what it is."

I don't know who said it, but someone chimed in, "I wish I knew he was betting on the Yankees. I would have bet the Tigers. I could have used the money."

"Who you got tonight, Chooch?" somebody asked.

"I'm not sure. I gotta do some handicapping."

The same voice said, "That's some handicapped handicapping."

I noticed a female carrier. She was blonde and a little chunky but in all the right places. The punch clock was right in front of the business routes, and they were already sorting mail. The clock must have hit 6:30 because the carriers were punching in. Carriers would punch in and go straight to their routes as if they were possessed. No more talking or chit chat. I punched in and Stanley informed me that I would be walking with Eugene. Route #22, the numbered streets.

Eugene walked past me and didn't say anything so I followed him to the route. Again, the routes were not in sequential order. Route 22 was between 19 and 37. About two feet from the route, Eugene stopped and just stood there as if in a trance. I assumed he might be praying as his lips were moving, but no sound was emanating from him. His eyes were closed.

Maybel was on route 19 and she noticed me watching this ordeal. She smiled and I must say her smile was as awesome as her breasts. She whispered to me, "He does this every day."

Even Stegman walked by and just rolled his eyes. Stegman commented to me, "Hey, nice shoes."

I asked Maybel, "Weren't you on a different route yesterday?"

She explained to me as she moved mail around her. "I'm a floater. I'm here when the guys get their day off. I do the same five routes, different routes every day, but the same sequence. You see, if you are off Monday this week, then you would be off on Tuesday next week. Then Wednesday the following week, and so on. Our work week ends on a Friday and starts on Saturday so every six weeks you get Friday for the week that past and Saturday for the upcoming week. But you pay for it with what we call the six bagger. You have to work Monday through Saturday straight through. Six days in a row and then you get Sunday and Monday off."

By this time, Eugene came out of his trance. He said to me, "Okay, our route is the numbered streets. It goes from Eleventh Street down to First Street. Windsor Parkway runs right down the middle of each street. Windsor divides each street into two loops, the high loop and the low loop. My advice to you is do not case Windsor and make a pile. When you have time, rack Windsor on its own, it will be faster."

"I'm open for suggestions," I said. He then told me to start on the letters, and he would do the flats. Of course, the first two letters were for Windsor Parkway. I ignored Eugene's advice and tried to rack them. I was searching the case and Eugene noticed. I guess I was taking too long.

"I thought you were open for suggestions? Make a pile with Windsor. Trust me, it is going to be easier."

I don't know why, but I lied and told him, "I'm studying the case. Mick told me to study the case first."

"Real easy," Eugene said, "Eleventh Street down to First Street. High numbers first, then low. Not much to study." I started casing and was getting the hang of it. And I had to admit that it was so much easier Eugene's way. Also, I noticed that when I scanned the letter for the address, if I said the address in my head "2 Fifth Street," it would help me with racking and prevent me from mis-racking. Sometimes, even though it was 2 Fifth Street, my hand would go towards Second Street.

After forty minutes I was getting much faster. Still slow, but for me, faster. Eugene ran out of flats and told me that he was going to sweep flats. He had a couple of misrouted flats that were for other routes, and he put them in the kickback case. He then proceeded to the other side of the building, the clerk side. Eugene finished and had Stanley count them. He handed me the flats and said," Flat time." Under his breath I heard him say, "So we can get out of here sometime today." I felt that was unnecessary. But then I saw him racking letters, and the letters were just flying into the case. I went about my business racking flats, and every now and then I heard something being said at the route next to me, route 37. I went back to racking and I heard it again. I swear that I heard the guy say "penis."

About three minutes went by, and I distinctly heard this guy say, "penis family." This day and a half that I had been working here at Farmingburg Post Office had been like a warped dream. These guys and events can only be described as kooky, weird, and bizarre. This cannot be real. I figured maybe at break time I would ask Eugene what this guy was saying, although this guy was not talkative and the only advice that he gave me was about racking Windsor Parkway. It was then that Mick walked past me and said, "Hey J, let's do a final flat sweep."

Eugene said, "Good idea." I wasn't keen on seeing the clerks. They were like real-life clowns and were somewhat intimidating. There was something really sinister about them. It was then that Mick told me that Roddy was walking with him today. He told me that I was a much better racker than Roddy.

He then said, "I hope I don't get that other new guy tomorrow. No offense, but you new guys slow me down."

"None taken," I retorted; and it dawned on me that I hadn't seen Hartman yet today. I wondered if he might have gotten fired or quit.

We approached the clerk section, and the first person that we saw was Suzy Forecast. I swear that she had on more make-up than yesterday, which was hard to believe. "Hello Mick, hello Mr. Johnson. There is a 40% chance of rain and possible thundershowers. The front will move in later today, but you should bring your rain gear just in case."

Mick quipped, "Suzy, all good carriers know how to walk between the raindrops."

Suzy just laughed and said, "Better safe than sorry."

Gordon, the 6-foot six-inch clerk, got riled up. "Yeah, but you ain't good, Mick. You probably catch more rain." Today, Flacco was not moving and his eyes were closed. I found out later he came to the Post Office straight from his other job as a bartender. He claimed that he made more money bartending than he did at the Post Office. And he was only here for the health benefits. Next up was Robard, and all I could think of was, *Who dresses this guy or why doesn't somebody say something?* The guy was wearing purple pants and a pink shirt. The guy up next, Joe, seemed like a normal guy and asked Mick how he thought the football Giants were going to do in the upcoming season. Mick said that he was optimistic because the draft went really well; and barring injuries, they should be able to turn it around. But every team had hope right now.

On our way to get Stanley to count our mail, I mentioned to Mick that the guy on route 37 says penis every couple of minutes. Mick laughed and said," That's my man Theo. He has a customer on his route named Phillip Ennis. He tells me to say the name fast with a hard second P. Phillip Ennis, Phil up penis. Sometimes the letter is addressed to P. Ennis or the P. Ennis family. So what you hear is just Theo having fun. This job is so mindless and mundane. You have to entertain yourself or become an alcoholic or go insane. Speaking of entertainment, make sure you see the Stegman hat dance today at break time."

Speaking of crazy, since I started this job I felt like I was on the brink. Stanley counted our flats and I told Mick that I would see him later. I got back to route 22 just in time to hear Theo say

"P Ennis and family." Then I heard a horn honk and somebody yelled, "Break time!" Someone else yelled, "Roach coach is here."

The carriers, like lemmings, headed for the doors to the loading dock. Some had their coffee cup in hand and were beelining to the breakroom. Others headed out to smoke and some to the comfy confines of their cars. I saw Roddy and asked him how he was doing. He told me that he didn't like Mick's route. He said he found it confusing. Now I had an idea of what Mick was talking about. I asked if he saw Yo-yo or if he heard anything about him. He started going on about him slipping and having to go to the doctor. I told him that I was well aware of that. I asked him if he had heard any updates. I then mentioned that it was my turn to pay from the coffee truck.

The coffee truck guy smiled and said hello, then added, "Hey, you got new shoes. I have the same ones, nice memory foam shoes." I looked down and noticed that he did indeed have the same shoes.

It was then that I heard it, "Yo, yo, yo, waz up guys, yo?" Hartman limped up to the truck with a boot on his foot.

Roddy greeted him with, "Hello, Eric. How's your foot? Kevin is buying today." I'm thinking, *Eric? I didn't know that Yo-yo's first name was Eric. Also, I was hoping that I was only buying for bigmouth Roddy, not Eric the bottomless pit, too.* Roddy cordially got a banana and said that he had coffee inside. Yo-yo on the other hand got a Danish, a bag of chips, an egg sandwich, a soda, and a juice. The juice was for later he informed me. The wife didn't make him lunch. The coffee truck guy and I settled up.

Yo-yo was going on about his condition. He didn't have any broken bones, but there might be some ligament damage. He told us that they had him on light duty and how he might get a lawyer. Roddy chimed in " I'm so sorry to hear that, Eric. But let's head inside because I don't want to miss the hat dance that Mick was telling me about." So we headed back into the office; and although it wasn't quite as hot as yesterday, it was nice to get back inside with the air-conditioning cranking.

Yo-yo lagged behind us; and as we reached command central, Stanley's desk, Yo-yo sat right down. This kid had some pair of *cojones*, I tell you. Right behind us was the parcel section and the shelves were about five feet tall. Every day during break, Stanley called his wife. He'd go in the parcel section and during the call, he would pace back and forth. Stegman was about as tall as the shelves so all that you would see on our side of the shelves was the hat moving back and forth, seemingly by itself. The other carriers would comment, "It's alive," or "It's magic. The hat moves by itself."

Roddy snickered and Yo-yo commented, "Yo, snap, that is hilarious, yo." It was definitely funny. Suzy saw us looking and commented, "We should write a book about this."

After two minutes Stanley finished his call with a sappy voice, "Okay, poochie poo, have a great day. I'll see you later. Call me if you need me to bring anything home." I can't believe that I was intimidated by this little man who called his wife poochie-poo. Not anymore. Stanley came around the corner "What? You never seen a man show affection for his wife?" He then spotted Hartman, "Hey, look who it is. Good afternoon, Mr. Hartman You are aware that you were supposed to be here at 8:30?"

Yo-yo responded, "Good afternoon? Yo, it's not even 9:00, yo."

Stegman yelled, "Break is over, ladies." Two minutes later he called out, "Final sweep!"

Eugene suggested, "Let's see if you can finish the flats while I sweep." I may be wrong, but it seemed my boy Eugene might have a bit of an attitude. He seemed to be one of those quiet sarcastic types. Maybe he can say another prayer for me to rack faster. I was doing the best that I could. I heard carriers walking behind me to sweep as I tried to throw the flats faster. Eugene was back faster than I anticipated. He handed me the letters he just swept and told me that he would finish the flats.

It was then that I heard the sweetest sound. High heels, the accountable cart being pushed, and that melodic voice, "Hey, guys and girls," Lucy called out. All of a sudden there was a buzz, an energy in the air. God, she was so sexy. I was smitten. She went around having carriers sign for certified, registered mail, insured, and their keys, if needed. We were the last routes and it seemed an eternity until she got here. "Just your keys today, Eugene;" and as he was signing, Lucy commented, "Kevin, your *choose* are so nice. I guess I can't call you *choose* anymore."

I melted and said, "I guess not, Lucy." But I was thinking, *You can call me anything that you desire.* Eugene had the flats down in trays and told me that I could go use the restroom to wash up if I wanted to and that he would finish the letters. I agreed that I most definitely wanted to wash up. I was thinking, *What does he mean, if I want? Of course I do.* I realized that the next five or so hours with this guy was going to be interesting. So I headed to the head and then reminded myself of the awful experience there yesterday. That stench scarred my memory. I had to admit that while I, myself, was no bed of roses, this guy made the paint peel. I got to the restroom and, thank goodness, nobody was around. So I used the bathroom and washed my hands. Again, I was amazed at how dirty my hands were. I realized that Eugene and I were way ahead of schedule. Because we were way ahead, I figured that I would go visit Mick and Roddy.

I walked down the business aisle and saw that most of the guys were pulling down their racked mail. Most of the guys had skids of mail. I mean lots of mail. Some businesses get sacks of mail and some have those white tubs full of mail for one stop. Once again, the guys were focused on getting out and delivering. The carriers were making small talk and I was sure I heard someone say, "That's the guy that was wearing those ridiculous shoes." At the end of the row of letter cases, there was enough space to squeeze through to the next row of cases. Mick was racking letters and Roddy was awkwardly throwing flats.

Roddy stopped when he saw me, but Mick kept racking letters with lightning speed.

"Hey, amigos," I said in greeting.

Roddy commented, "This route is so confusing." I looked over at MacGregor's route and there was someone else there. As Roddy was still complaining, I asked Mick where his buddy the Scotsman was. "Oh, today is his day off. Good ol' Ray is his floater, the best floater ever. Ray is my floater, too. I'm off tomorrow. Ray will be doing my route. Ray's nickname is Dogbite. He got bit two times last year."

Ray corrected him. "Nope, that was three times last year and two the year before. I'm still waiting on the checks from last year to come in!"

Mick explained to me that if you happen to get bit by a dog, you end up suing the homeowners. You get lawyers involved and even if the skin is not broken, you still get paid. Trauma and all that. The Post Office had over 6,000 dog bites a year. Ray informed us that management wanted to write him up for getting bit by the dogs. "Like it's my fault," he said. Ray's wife suggested that he rub bacon on his legs so he gets bit again. She claimed that they needed a new kitchen and the roof needed repairs. Ray pulled up his pant leg, and right above his sock was a pretty nasty scar. He showed me his forearm and there was a slight scar. I took notice and wondered just how much Ray got paid. As if on cue, Ray said the last dog bite barely broke the skin and he was expecting two thousand dollars. Two G's? I could use two G's.

Mick changed the subject and asked, "How's it working with Eugene? Probably talking your ear off, huh?"

Ray laughed and said, "Let us pray."

I saw Stegman coming down the aisle, so I figured that I would head back to route 22. Eugene was pulled down and ready to go. He asked me, "Where were you?" I told him that I was talking to Mick and my friend Roddy. I mentioned that we were at least a half-hour ahead of schedule. And he asked, "

What's your point?" I wasn't sure if that was a rhetorical question so I didn't respond. He said that I could make myself useful if I went and got the parcels. "You do know where the parcel section is, don't you?" I'm telling you this guy was really pissing me off. I said that I did, so he told me to retrieve the parcels for route 22.

I went to the parcel section and Suzy Forecast was there. "Hello, Mr. Johnson," she said which was weird as I must have been 20 years her junior.

"Please call me Kevin."

Suzy then advised that the humidity could sneak up on you and to drink plenty of liquids so you don't get dehydrated. I thanked her and she smiled and asked, "Are you married, Kevin?" I don't know why, but I lied and told her no but that I had a serious girlfriend. I retrieved the parcels for route 22. Luckily, there were only four and they were not very large. As I made my way back, I noticed Nancy Cummings walking toward me. Again, she was wearing a business suit. I could be wrong but there might have been a slight smile of recognition.

As I turned into route 22, I heard Theo say, "P. Ennis and family." Cummings stopped and yelled. "Stegman, I need you right here, right now." Stegman came flying down the aisle, again amazing me at how fast this guy could move.

"Yes, Ms. Cummings?"

"He is doing it again. I'm a lady and should not be subjected to his filthy, obscene vulgarity."

To which Stanley replied, "Ms. Cummings, we discussed this with the Union. He is just reading the customer's name. He's really not doing anything wrong. The Union said they were not responsible for how you interpret it."

"Stegman, you know as well as me that he only does it when I am walking by, and he doesn't say any other customers' names."

Word must have gotten around about this situation, and somebody screamed across the room, "Phillip Ennis."

Cummings got all flustered and headed back to her office at which point you heard numerous guys yelling, "P. Ennis" or just penis. I thought I even heard a female voice.

Cummings was still saying, "This is sexual harassment. I could get you all written up. I am calling my contacts in Regional."

There were a couple more catcalls and Stanley started saying, "Alright you jackals, you've had your fun, now hush." At this point, Eugene was back and we wheeled the racked mail out to the loading dock. Eugene asked me if I got ALL the parcels and I assured him that I did. He told me to unload the cart and he would get the two-seater. The mail was neatly organized into five trays of rubber-banded letters and two trays of flats. As I put the mail on the loading dock, there was a big box truck backing up next to me. The truck was backing up way too fast but stopped abruptly two feet before the edge of the loading dock. The truck stopped and then backed up again and again, way too fast. The truck crashed into the loading dock with a thud. The loading dock had half tires as cushions, but this was a good collision. Floyd Lloyd was driving the truck, or was it Lloyd Floyd? Tim Waits was already backed in and said, "Atta boy, Floyd. You got it."

Floyd looked at me as he was getting out of his truck and said, "Smooooth." I was thinking, *If that is smooth, what kind of impact isn't?* Now Eugene was backing up and stopped with a foot to spare. He got out of the jeep and asked me, "Why didn't you bring the cart back inside?"

I'd had enough of this guy and retorted, "Did you ask me to bring the cart back inside, Gene?"

He quickly said, "It's Eugene." I knew full well he liked to be called Eugene. So I brought the cart inside, punched out for the street, and headed back out to the loading dock. My man Eugene was gone. At first, I thought he took that Gene thing way too hard and maybe he ditched me. Then I saw the two-seater out in the parking lot so I headed that way. As I was heading for the jeep, Eugene was heading back towards me. Angrily, he mentioned that we forgot to punch out. I told him not we, as I had already punched out. I walked back in the office with Eugene.

I heard over the loudspeaker, "Stan Stegman 1016. Stan Stegman 1016. Yo, oh sorry." Obviously, they had Yo-yo working the phones. Guys were yelling, "Yo, Stan, the phone, yo."

I smiled and headed out to the two-seater with my man, Gene. We drove in silence for about seven minutes. To break the silence, I asked him if it was hard to drive on the right-hand side. His response was, "No." I waited about a minute and popped the question, "Will I be able to drive the jeep today?" Again, his response was "No."

He made two turns and pulled up in between two houses on Windsor Parkway. He just stopped and reached behind into the back of the jeep and grabbed a couple of flats and letters that he had rubber-banded together. He jumped out of the jeep and ran up to the two houses and delivered their mail. He jumped back in the jeep and drove across a street that I realized was First Street. He pulled up to the next two houses on Windsor and again reached back, grabbed the mail, jumped out of the jeep, and proceeded to deliver the mail. We continued down Windsor, past Second Street, and he followed the same pattern until we got to the end, Eleventh Street.

Now, Eleventh Street only had houses on one side and there was a park on the other side. We were actually on the border of Farmingburg and the next town, Greenlawn. The other side of the park was where Greenlawn began. Eugene had each house individually rubber banded up. He fingered through the flats, jumped out, and delivered two houses at a time, just like Windsor Parkway. I let him know one of the parcels was for 15 Eleventh Street.

I think he mumbled, "Thanks." I've got to give it to my boy, he was really hustling along. I had to admit this was so much easier than yesterday where I was on my feet all day. I was just sitting here, going for a ride-along. I almost felt guilty as I was doing absolutely nothing. I thought about asking Eugene if there was anything that I could do to help. I decided against it because the man didn't have much of a vocabulary.

There were ten houses on this one-sided block, and all of them were split ranches. There were quite a few steps to go up to get where the mailboxes were located. Eugene was taking two steps at a time and was making good time. One house had a sprinkler on and Eugene went through it seemingly on purpose, maybe to cool off. The second to last house, number 15, had that parcel so Eugene went around to the back door of the jeep and retrieved it. He climbed the steps and knocked on the door. Less than a minute later a woman answered the door. They made chit chat, and Eugene entered the house. I was just sitting there waiting, and a short time later Eugene came out carrying two bottles of water. When he got in the jeep he just said, "Here" and gave me one of the bottles. He then added if a customer offered you a drink, take it. He explained that they were reluctant to offer again if you turned them down. He then drove to the last house and delivered their mail. Because we were at a dead-end, Eugene made a u-turn. There was nothing but woods at the end of the block. We headed back to Windsor Parkway and Eugene jumped out to do the south side of Windsor as we had already done the north side when we came up Windsor. When he climbed back into the jeep, he suddenly drove across Windsor and pulled up to the first house on the corner of Tenth Street.

I'M A MAILMAN

15 Tenth Street. He reached in the back where there was an old, worn-out mailbag. He handed me the bag without saying a word. He then handed me a bundle of flats and three bundles of letters. "Start at 15 and go down the odds. Well, pretty much just follow the mail," was all he said. Alrighty then, I'm going to be a letter carrier. Let's do this. Eugene zoomed away across Windsor to do the other loop on Tenth Street. I began as I climbed the steps of 15 Tenth Street. I got to the top step and put the letters and flats in the mailbox. I then proceeded to number 13. I got to the top step and was looking for the mailbox but did not see one. I looked around and saw a brass mail slot in the door. I opened the storm door and put the mail in. I turned and walked down the steps. I was feeling pretty good. It was a nice sunny day and I felt free. I really enjoyed being outdoors, especially on such a nice day. It was so much better than being in the office. I did a couple more houses and was near the end of the odd-numbered houses. I went up the steps to number 3. There was an overgrowth of bushes and as I headed up the steps, I felt something on my face. I realized that it was cobwebs as I pulled them away. I headed up the steps and hoped the spider who made the cobweb was nowhere around. I deposited the mail and

headed down the steps, still brushing my clothes as I went to the last house, number 1. I then crossed the street to number 2 and headed up the even side. At 6 Tenth Street, there was a dog in a fenced-in area. He was up on his two hind legs and wagging his tail. I stopped to pet him and, of course, said, "Who's a good boy," not even knowing if it was a boy or a girl. I had about four houses to go when I saw Eugene pulling up at the end of my loop.

Dang, I was hoping that I would finish before him. After all, he had to drop me off, drive across Windsor, do his loop, then drive back to pick me up. As I picked up my pace, I realized this was not skilled labor. Anybody who could walk could do this job. I mean, there was not much more to learn, rack the mail, deliver the mail. When delivering, just follow the sequence. I finished the loop and jumped in the jeep. Eugene started the jeep and turned on Windsor. He drove past the two houses between Tenth and Ninth so I asked him why, and he told me he already did them.

He said, "I saw you petting 'Ringworm' and knew that I had plenty of time to do the Windsor Parkway houses. I was shocked that he had that much time and I inquired, "Ringworm?"

Eugene seemed almost human when he laughed and said, "Don't worry, you're not going to catch anything from him. He was a stray and had sores all over his body. He's fine now but the name stuck. He's one of the coolest dogs I have ever come across." He then became the old Eugene when he added, "I finished my loop. What was I supposed to do with all that time? I'm not the type to sit around and do absolutely nothing." He proceeded to Ninth Street and dropped me off. He quickly did his u-turn and headed across Windsor Parkway. I was determined to finish this loop and be waiting for this guy when he got here. I headed up to the first house, 17 Ninth Street. The loop seemed to be getting larger. Although it was the same sequence— head down the odds and up the evens. When I got to 7 Ninth Street, I noticed that I have mail racked for 9 Seventh

Street so I couldn't deliver those letters. I crossed the street to deliver the even numbers. At 6 Ninth Street, I had a letter for 9 Sixth Street. At 10 Ninth Street, there is a letter in the mailbox. It was not outgoing mail but was a misdelivered letter. The letter was for 9 Tenth Street and written on the envelope the customer wrote "We live on Tenth Street, this letter is for Ninth Street. Please deliver to the correct address next time." I wondered how many times this had happened.

    I remembered that earlier in the office guys would comment to Eugene about his "get to know your neighbor policy." I imagine this was what they were referring to. I found out later that if a customer called to complain, the Supervisor would blow them off by telling them what they wanted to hear just to get them out of his hair. I was two houses away from the end of the loop, and he did it again. Eugene was waiting for me. When I jumped in the jeep, I showed Eugene the misracked mail. He told me that I needed to be more careful when I racked the mail. I then showed him the misdelivered mail with the comment on it, and he just snatched the mail out of my hand and drove off onto Windsor. Apparently, my man Eugene cannot accept the fact that he was wrong. I mean, I could have misracked some of the mail, but he definitely misdelivered the mail yesterday. I didn't think that I made that mistake. There was an awkward silence as he drove past the houses on Windsor. Apparently, he delivered to those already.

    Eugene dropped me off at the next loop on the corner of Eighth Street. Without a word, he did his u-turn and headed off to his loop. I was determined to be done with my loop before him. I was focused, climbing steps sometimes two at a time. I hopped over a hedge and was making really good time. There were, of course, a misrack or two and one misdelivery. I crossed over to the even numbers and was so confident I got Eugene this time. At number 8, the door was open and a woman was in the doorway wearing a bathing suit. She was attractive, very tan, and in phenomenal shape. A little older, maybe early forties. She commented that it was very warm out and offered me a drink, "perhaps an adult beverage?" I remembered what I was taught earlier that day to not turn down customers when they offered a drink and I asked, "Do you have iced tea?"

The lady said "I'm pretty sure. By the way, I'm Elise Hightower. I don't think I've seen you before."

I replied, "Well, today is only my second day. It's nice to meet you, Ms. Hightower."

"Please call me Elise, Can I ask you something? Do you know Bobby Lamore?"

I responded, "I don't really know him personally, but I know who he is."

Elise told me, "The reason that I ask is that he had this route 10 years ago, and I haven't seen him in a while."

It dawned on me that she probably is, or actually was, one of Lamore's conquests. I noticed that her house was immaculately decorated and told Elise that she did a wonderful job. She handed me the iced tea and thanked me. I realized that I was very thirsty. I gulped it down and it dawned on me that Eugene was probably waiting on me. Elise commented that I was drinking way too fast. She told me one of her jobs was as a freelance masseuse. I picked up my raggedy mailbag and Elise handed me her business card. I flew out the door and Elise waved goodbye. I had five houses to do and Eugene was already waiting.

I finished the loop and jumped in the jeep. I apologized to Eugene for being late as I handed him the misracks. I informed him that Ms. Hightower offered me a drink, and I took her up on it. I asked him if he ever took her up on a massage. Eugene barked at me, "Hey, I'm married, and happily at that, and you know she charges." I was thinking, *Of course she doesn't do it for free.* Again, he said and emphasized, "SHE CHARGES." Then it hit me. He was implying that she was a pro. Then I wondered to myself, *How much does she charge?* Hey, it was a multibillion-dollar business, I doubted that I was the only guy who would consider it. To tell the truth, I would rather get a foot massage right now than any hanky panky. But I made a mental note, 8 Eighth, and I made sure I still had her business card.

So Eugene dropped me off at Seventh Street, and I was determined this was the loop where I beat his ass. To no avail, but I was close. He dropped me off on Sixth Street, and I realized five more loops and we were done. The temperature was rising, and I was beginning to perspire. We were way more than halfway done and it was only 11:30 a.m. I was really making good time, but I still had two houses when he pulled up. As he dropped me off at Fifth, my resolve had not wavered. I would beat him. I was doing well. I was about to finish the odds as I fingered the letters for 1 Fifth Street. There was an important letter for number 3, the house I just delivered to. I backtracked and returned to 3, After all, that's what I would want my letter carrier to do. So, I finished the odd side, headed over to the even, and missed him by one house. I figured a moral victory as I went back to house number 3. Fourth Street and Third Street. He beat me again.

I was coming close and only had two loops to beat him, Second and First Streets. Going from Third to Second Street, he stopped on Windsor to deliver. I was coming closer. He didn't have the time to do Windsor anymore. Second Street was a tie. I was coming down the steps of the last house as he pulled up. He stopped on Windsor to deliver the two houses. As we drove to the last loop on First, Eugene let me know that one of the houses had a letter that was backward. The backward letter indicated that that house had a small parcel. The parcel looks like a box of checks. Last chance to beat this guy. I moved down the odd side like lightning. At 7, I delivered the small parcel. I crossed to the even side. I saw from across the street a guy coming out of 5 heading towards his car and he waved. I waved back. I was thinking, *Please do not slow me down by asking a question,* which he didn't.

I had about four houses to go when that same guy drove up

to me and honked. He waved a letter at me as I came down the steps of number 10. He said, " Excuse me, but I live at 7 First Street and this letter is for 1 Seventh Street." I apologized to the gentleman. He laughed and said that it happened all the time. "Eugene does it quite often. If it looks important, we bring it to the other people's house ourselves. We have called to complain, but nothing seems to get done about it. I have actually made a couple of friends by bringing them their mail. People I normally would not have interacted with otherwise. We accept it by now. My only concern is if unscrupulous people get their hands on something important. Or somebody might throw the mail away."

I understood the gentleman's concern. Well, this miscue is on me. I was more concerned with beating Eugene than concentrating on getting the proper mail delivered. I might not have misracked the mail, but I definitely misdelivered it. I finished the loop and walked away from the last house and jumped into the jeep. Eugene was smiling and said, "We are done, amigo. Yeah, man, that's another one in the books. Are you hungry? We will go to my house for lunch."

What's become of this guy? It was as if he avoided conversation all day. Now he was talking up a storm. Eugene drove back up Windsor towards Eleventh Street. He told me to visualize the case for the route. He mentioned that on the case, each loop would start with a house on Windsor Parkway. The loop would then go down the lower street numbers, do a house on Windsor, cross the street to do another house on Windsor, then do the high numbers on the street. Finally, the loop would end on Windsor and you would cross the parkway to end up where you started. Eugene told me he pulled it down his way which was faster and easier. Of course, he mentioned that if you ever get walked by a supervisor or management, you always do it the way it is on the case, the slow way.

I wanted to take advantage of his talkative status so I asked, "How often does a route get walked?"

Eugene said that we were supposed to get walked once a year. Ironically, he said, "The week before we get walked, we see an increase in bulk mail. The day we are walked, there is virtually no bulk mail. Magically, the bulk mail disappears. It's nonexistent. Of course, when the inspections are over, the bulk mail reappears with a vengeance. Every day is different. Management assumes that if you can do a route real fast one day that you would be able to duplicate that rate every day. There are so many intangibles delivering to three hundred houses a day. Every day is not the same no matter what management thinks. Plus, if we did everything that we are supposed to do according to the M-41, we would never finish. According to the carrier handbook, the M-41, we are supposed to turn the jeep wheels towards the curb EVERY TIME we park. Chock the wheels every time. Are you serious?"

I asked him when I was going to get an M-41.

Eugene laughed and said, "In the ten years I've worked at the Post Office, I've never even seen one. Management uses information in it against us. Letterman is always quoting from it. That's a really good question. Where do we get one? I guess ask Letterman for one. You never answered my question, are you hungry?"

I didn't realize it but, "Yes I am," I replied.

It was only 12:20 and we had some time to kill, about two and a half hours. I was thinking, *This is awesome!* Eugene mentioned that he usually made up time every day. He pointed out that I did about 40 percent of the route today. But he was usually done by 1:00 on most days. He added that although it seemed like a long break, his time included a half-hour lunch that we did not get paid for. This also included a fifteen-minute break, and we busted our asses to get it.

I asked Eugene, "Where are we going to eat?" He repeated that we were going to his house and his wife would have something good for us.

"I never buy lunch out. It is very expensive. I got two kids and a mortgage. Basically, I have much better things to do with my money."

I asked him, "Wow, you really live here in Farmingburg? I imagine it's a very easy commute."

"Dude, six minutes if I get all the red lights. I read somewhere If you want less stress in your life, live twenty minutes or less from where you work. I have neighbors who work in downtown Manhattan. Their day starts by driving to the railroad station trying to find a parking space. Then a forty-minute train ride, if the train is on time. They get off the train and then have to catch either the subway or a cab downtown. The cost is well over $500 a month just for travel and the parking permit for the train station. Then they have to come home an hour and a half each way. My neighbor Mike is wiped out every day. He has a 14-hour day. No thanks." Eugene explained that he and the missus bought a house on Hampshire Drive eight years ago and he loved it. He was happy with the school and his neighbors. Eugene said his major complaint was the Long Island taxes which were ridiculously high. I was only somewhat familiar with Farmingburg, and there were houses on the hill that were more high end than the numbered streets. I was curious and asked, "You live in the hills?" Eugene told me that he did.

"My wife works for the railroad. Trust me, I couldn't afford that house on a letter carrier salary." I told Eugene that I had applied to the railroad as an electronic troubleshooter. He told me, "Good luck. It's hard to get in, lots of nepotism. Their union is strong. They literally have the power to shut the city down. Our union is pretty much a joke. My wife is an engineer."

I was taken back. "She really drives the train?"

He told me that she did and earned almost triple what he made. "And forget about it. If she works an overtime shift, she makes more in sixteen hours than I do all week." It's really sad. He explained that his wife Johanna worked a four to midnight shift. She loves it and loves her hours since she can go to the gym before work. She loved her job and said that it was really easy to drive the train, just regulate the speed and start and stop at the train stations. To make the train go, they press a bar down. Eugene came home about 3:15 and Johanna would then leave for work. She would drive to the Farmingburg train station and jump on the train to take her to work. At that time, most of the trains were leaving Manhattan taking the Long Islanders home. Eugene had dinner with the kids and put them to bed. Johanna gets the kids off to school.

Eugene never worked overtime. He did his eight house and leaves. Most days he could get out on time and sometimes he would eat fifteen to twenty minutes if he was late. Other times, if he was really late, he would give away a piece of his route to another carrier for overtime or just regular work for the lowly PTFs. Every route was broken down to five one-hour pieces. You could find the breakdowns in the route book. I made a mental note of this info.

LIVING LARGE

We got to Eugene's house and wow, this guy was living large. I mean, this was a really nice house. The lawn was well manicured, a good size, and I was amazed. There was a new model Mercedes in the driveway. We proceeded inside and I was introduced to Johanna. Again, I was blown away. What a cutie, extremely attractive, nice figure, and gorgeous smile. How lucky can one guy be? His kids, a boy and a girl, came in from the in-ground pool. They said, "Hello, sir" and hugged and kissed Eugene. He offered me a beer so I asked, "Are you going to have one?" Eugene said no, but I thought, *End of the day, and I'm not driving. Screw it.* "Yes, I will take you up on that and have a beer." I sat in the dining room as Johanna made sandwiches. I finished my beer when she served the sandwich. This goddess had another beer for me.

Johanna asked me if I was married. So I told her no and that I was recently discharged from the Army and just got back to Long Island from Texas. Johanna yelled to Eugene, "Hey, Eugene, we can set Kevin up with my friend, Miriam."

"Crazy Miriam? I'm not sure he would be able to handle her," Eugene responded.

I said," I might be up for a challenge." I told Johanna that I put in for the Long Island Rail Road as an electronic technician.

"Oh, yeah, the guys that work on the track switches. Well good luck with that," she said. Eugene and Johanna went about their business, and I sat in front of the television with *Sportscenter* on and the air-conditioning cranking.

I was totally envying Eugene's life—beautiful house, beautiful wife, great kids—what more could anyone want or need? Suddenly, a big beautiful standard poodle walked in and sat down right next to me as I thought, *That's what more a guy can ask for, a great dog.* So I pet the dog, finished my beer, and watched TV. I was totally relaxed and realized that I hadn't seen Eugene or Johanna in twenty or thirty minutes. The little boy came in and yelled, "Mom!" The poodle just raised his or her head but otherwise didn't move.The little boy said, "I see you met Newman." The boy introduced himself as Clifford and sat down. "What's your favorite type of dog?" I told him that I liked friendly dogs; and if they were smart, I liked them more. I swear Newman seemed to pay attention.

Cliff informed me that Newman was a really smart dog. I said, "That's probably why we get along so well." Eugene came out from the back and he had changed his postal shirt to a navy blue t-shirt. It appeared he may have taken a shower, too.

Cliff asked Eugene "Where's mom?" Johanna came from out back, and her hair was a bit disheveled. It finally dawned on me, Oh shoot, they got in a quicky. Made sense because she would be going to work soon. I was so jealous, I felt like I had a good day and this guy had all good days. Eugene told me that we would be leaving soon. I mentioned that was a good idea because I was thinking of moving in. Not that I had any say in the matter.

I said goodbye to Clifford and Newman, and Johanna gave me a hug and said, "Good luck in your new career."

I reminded her, "I'm planning on working with you soon." Johanna laughed. I told Eugene that he was one lucky son of a gun. Eugene, of course, was waiting for me in the jeep, not the first time today.

A five-minute drive back to the Post Office. Eugene backed up to the loading dock, I don't know why. We only had empty trays and maybe ten letters and two misracked flats. I brought the empty trays back to route 22. Mike the Mortician and the love of my life, Lucy Consuelo, were sitting at the supervisor's desk laughing. Damn, whenever they were together they were laughing. That's right, I was jealous. There was a tray of mail near the desk, and Lucy said to Mike, "Hey, maybe Kevin wants to do the piece."

"Good idea, Loose. Loose, he called her Loose, I think I hate him. So Mike asked me, "Do you want some O.T., Johnson?"

I told him, "Sure, but how do I get there?" At this point, Eugene was walking into the office. "Take the two seater. It's on route 17. You can check the route book on how to get there." I went to route 17 and checked the map.

I made a mental note to go down Main Street and make a right on Junard Boulevard, proceed to Davidson Avenue, and begin. I was so excited to finally be driving a right-hand sided vehicle. I took the mail and started driving down Main Street. I was pretty disappointed with the right-hand side driving. It was pretty much the same, just different proportions. I made my right on Junard, and Davidson Avenue was right there. I parked the jeep but did not chock the wheels towards the curb. It seemed stupid. There were five loops and I was done. No incidents, but at least four customers commented, "You're late. Where's Pete the Greek?" I told them it was my second day on the job and I did not know Pete. My remark did not seem to help their attitude, like I was personally screwing them.

I looked at my watch and saw that it was a couple of minutes before 4:00. I was going to be way later than an hour. There was a little bit of traffic going back to the office. I pulled up to "ye old Farmingburg Post Office" and parked the two-seater. I rushed into the office and saw Joey Rags. He asked me, "How's it going?" I told him they gave me an hour piece and it was more than an hour. Joey laughed and said, "Pfff, no problem. Tell Stegman, if he asks, travel time." I brought the misracks over to route 17 and opened the route book. It seemed I was doing more than an hour on route 17. They threw in an extra block.

I saw Mike the Mortician and he waved me over. I was a tad nervous and I told him the piece was an extra street and therefore longer than an hour. Mike said "Don't worry about it." He then thanked me for helping him out by delivering the mail. He informed me that Stegman had me coming in at 8:30 a.m. to walk Dittmeyer's route. I told Mike that I would be at work at 8:30. I was starting to appreciate Mike. Notice I did not say I liked him.

I saw Lucy at the window and she smiled and waved to me. My heart melted, and I felt all warm and fuzzy inside. I went to the bathroom to wash up and I noticed that I was getting quite a bit of sun. My face and my arms were all red. I recalled the carrier who believed that the Post Office should supply sunscreen and concurred that they should. I was in no hurry to punch out. I felt I had to make up for the 45-minute orientation time yesterday where we listened to Stanley rant without being on the clock. I left the bathroom and was on the Post Office floor. The afternoons were so different than the mornings. The cases were empty, and there was no mail on the floor. There was so much less energy. Even the carriers were more laid back, not possessed like the morning. There were no clerks in the kickback area, and it was quiet. So I went to the punch-out clock. There were a couple of carriers waiting to punch out and go home.

One of them, a Ski Boy, said, "Hey, J."

I replied, "Hey." I could not remember his name. It was coming to me. "Where's Your House Key," I remembered they called him.

He asked me, "You going to the Morbid Obesity show Saturday night?"

Another carrier came in and said, "Hey, Chris." I

remembered, *That's right, Chris Wojohowski was his name.* I replied that I most certainly would make an effort and told him that I was working on Sunday. Before he answered, I heard the loudspeaker: "Nancy Cummings 1016, Yo, Nancy Cummings 1016." Chris told me that Sunday was really easy. It was over before you knew it. You emptied mailboxes and went to Regional to pick up express mail; and if there was express for a residential customer, you delivered it. He added that you got time and a quarter and would probably be done before two hours. You didn't punch out and Stegman would sign you out for two hours. I was relieved to find out it was going to be less than two hours. I asked Chris who usually went because if Lucy was there so was I.

He said, "You never know, but it's always cool to see our co-workers outside this dump. Me and Joey Ramonski are kind of like roadies. We set up and break down the stage and equipment. The guys are getting quite a following. The place gets packed."

"I'm glad you brought that up. Where are they playing?" He told me the Modern bar right here on Main Street.

Quentin came in from the street and said, "Where's Your House Key, waz up, buddy?"

Chris said, "Hey, Q."

All of a sudden, Yo-yo came around by the carrier desk. "Yo, yo, yo. Hey Kev, I got you a sweet deal for tomorrow. You're coming in at 8:30, yo. And all you gotta do is walk Dittmeyer's route, yo."

Quentin said, "I love this kid. Waz up Yo-yo?"

Hartman responded, "Hey Quentin, they are going to get you those two hours off that you requested for Friday."

Q just said, "Oh, yeah."

Hartman turned to me. "Yo, Kev, you will be walking Ditt's route, route 38 when you come in at 8:30, yo."

"I already know, Yo-yo."

"Who told you, Kev?"

"Mike did."

"Whoa, I wanted to tell you."

I was thinking, *How did this guy become so involved in the administrative goings on?* Again, I didn't think postal management was skilled labor either. But seriously, Yo-yo making decisions? How did this idiot become so involved?

Then he hit me with, "Yo, Kev, do you think you can give me a ride home, yo?"

I asked him, "When are you leaving?"

"Whenever you do, yo." I told him I was punching out in ten minutes. "Yo, I'm there, yo."

I punched out ten minutes later and sat and waited and waited. I was watching carriers come in from the street. I considered leaving a couple of times but talked myself out of it. Fifteen minutes after I punched, out my man Eric, Yo-yo, Hartman graced me with his presence. He finally punched out, and we were walking past the loading dock as Floyd Lloyd was backing up. BAM, he hit the loading dock pretty good.

Yo-yo was blabbering about postal management. Blah, blah, the PM this, blah, blah the SPO that. I wasn't listening and did not care. It suddenly dawned on me that I did not have a clue where Yo-yo lived. I interrupted him to ask. He responded, "Yo, Babylon, yo, not far from here. Ten minutes." I realized this guy had no real time reality. He must live at least twenty minutes away. Of course, it was the opposite direction that I was heading. Also, it was 5:00 p.m. so we would definitely hit traffic. The drive took us 30 minutes. When we got near his house, he dropped the bomb on me. "Yo, since I got you that sweet deal tomorrow, yo, and we both gotta be in at 8:30, do you think you can drive me in tomorrow? My old lady is pregnant, yo, and she would have to bring the other kids, yo. And yo, we only have one car."

Just so I didn't have to hear him say "yo" anymore, I told him, "Yes I will be here tomorrow at 8:00."

He questioned, "Eight o'clock? Isn't that kinda early? Shouldn't you come at 8:15?"

I explained, "We are still brand new and on probation. Let's not cut it so close. I like to be at work early."

"Why?" he asked.

"That's the kind of guy I am. I was raised that way."

I thought I saw an eye roll. "Yo, why don't you come in and meet the fam, yo."

I let him know that I was in a hurry, a lie. He got out of the car and a young boy around three came running out the house.

He yelled, "Daddy" and jumped in his arms. An older woman was at the door with a toddler at her feet. And from the street you could see that she was pregnant.

Hartman said, "Babe, this is Kev. We started together yesterday. He's my new best friend."

WHAT? Best friends? I barely knew this guy, and I didn't really like him. Why did I have to be his best friend?

His wife opened the door and I said, "Nice to meet you, Ms. Hartman."

She said, "Hi, it's my pleasure, but please call me Gladys." Not to be judgemental, but Gladys was in her mid thirties and Yo-yo was only early twenties. Gladys invited me in and let me know that it was a little messy. "Why don't you stay for dinner?"

I told her that I appreciated the offer but I had a couple of things to do and should be going. "Perhaps another time," I said. She smiled and waved goodbye.

I jumped in my car. I wanted to get a six pack of brewskis, take a shower, and watch the Yankees game. I wish I knew who Chooch bet on. I got home, cracked a few beers, and ate a slice that I picked up on the way home. I was watching the game, and before I knew it it was 5:00 a.m. I was in my chair with half a beer next to me. What a waste. I brushed my teeth and went to bed. Thank goodness that I didn't have to be at work until 8:30. Man, I wish I didn't have to pick up Yo-yo.

DAY 3: ALL BY MYSELF

My alarm went off at 7:00, and my very first thought was that I could have slept another half hour if I did not have to pick up Yo-yo. Also, I was feeling the effects of all the walking over the past couple of days. Nothing major, just a little stiffness and soreness. I showered and dressed for work and jumped in my car. I drove to the Hartman residence, or as Yo-yo said, "My new best friend," God help me. It was 7:57 when I pulled up and honked the horn. And I waited. I honked the horn again at 7:59 and I figured I would be best served to go up and knock. It was exactly 8:00 when I knocked on the door. As I was waiting, I looked for the doorbell. There it was, so I rang the doorbell and knocked. And I waited some more. So I rang the bell and knocked again. At this juncture, I was debating whether I stay or go. I rang the bell and knocked really loud. I heard Yo-yo say, "Yo, who is it?" *For real, who is it?*

I said the postal police as a joke. Yo-yo opened the door and he was in his underwear.

"Yo, what time is it? Yo." I informed him that it was 8:02 and we had to be at work in twenty-something minutes, and it was at least a twenty-minute ride and he better move his ass. Yo-yo assured me that he would be ready in five minutes. I remembered that yesterday's five minutes was at least fifteen minutes.

"Yo, like, I'm not going to have time to shower or eat? Yo."

"You can do both of those, but you're going to need a ride to work," I told him. I saw the three-year-old behind him in the living room. He invited me in and I don't know why, but I accepted and went inside. I probably went to make sure he didn't do anything stupid like go back to bed or start cooking. I sat in the living room and the little guy came in and I said hello. The little guy didn't respond but waved to me. Just like Gladys said, the house was messy. Not dirty, but toys and stuff all over the place.

Yo-yo was finally ready to go. I was afraid to look at my watch but I saw that it was 8:22. Damn, I was going to be late on my onliest (what my man Catfish would say) third day on the job. And it was because of this moron. On the drive in, Yo-yo implied that it was Gladys's fault that he was late. She was up late, sick from the pregnancy. I told him that we were new and they were kind of big on punctuality. I drove pretty quickly and we arrived at the Post Office at 8:37. I rushed across the street to try and minimize how late we were.

I punched in and as I turned around there was Stegman. "Good afternoon, Johnson. I wasn't sure if you were coming to work this wonderful day. I see you did some overtime yesterday."

"Yes, Stan. Mike the Mor.., I mean Mike sent me out with a piece on route 17 when I came back."

"It was my understanding that it was an hour piece."

I told him, "I think it was a little more, and then travel time, and I wasn't sure where I was going."

Stegman snorted, "Yeah, well, you milked it for an hour and forty minutes overtime." What? Was the money coming out of his pocket? At this time Yo-yo came strolling in. Man, was I glad to see my new best friend! Stanley turned to address Yo-yo, and I made my way over to Dittmeyer's route.

"Hey, Ditt, last day. Boy, am I jealous."

"Look, youngblood, do not wish your life away. If this is what you decide to do with the rest of your life, then God bless you. Good luck, try to enjoy the journey. Okay, the flats are down. I've got a few more letters to rack. You can go see Lucy at the window. You need to sign for the keys and there is some certified mail. On Lafayette Street there's a box you need to empty."

"I'm on it, Ditt," I said. I was going to see Lucy. Not only that, I was going to see what she wore. I was going to smell her perfume. Man, I was beginning to sound like MONA. I needed to get some. So I went to the window and there she was, as beautiful as ever.

Lucy saw me, smiled, and asked, "What can I do to help you, Kevin?" *Oh, you don't want to know*, I thought to myself. I told her that I was covering Ditt's route today. That sweet thing said, "Oh, I am so happy for him!" While she was retrieving the keys and certified mail for me, I was next to the doorway to the counter, you know, where you go to buy stamps, weigh and send packages, put mail on hold, and so on. It was a few minutes before 9:00 a.m., and there was a line of about five people. There were two clerks who were attending to these customers. These clerks were wearing collared shirts and ties and looked professional. The clerk closest to me apparently finished with his customer as the customer left. He was still busy with his head down tying up loose ends from the last transaction. The next customer walked up to his counter and the clerk looked up and said, "I didn't call you yet." He then waved his hand at the customer shooing him back to the line. The customer went back to the beginning of the line and the clerk finished whatever he was doing. He then looked up and said, "Next." The customer then went back to the counter he was at just a few seconds before.

By this time, Lucy had my keys and accountables. "I don't like when he does that," Lucy said. "I don't know if it's a power thing, but the people get angry and make them think negatively about the Post Office. When customers think about the Post Office, they think of the carriers and the clerks at the counter. They don't know or think about workers like me. But that's what he does." If she only knew that I thought about her. I told her she was such a bright spot in such a dreary environment. Lucy smiled and had me sign for the keys.

The clerk section was empty. I think they were at lunch. At this section of the building was the window, counter, a vault, and a couple of offices. There was a desk with a phone which I found out was the clerk supervisor's desk. It also was strategically placed so he could oversee the clerks' work. I wondered if he could see when Gordon was sleeping. I saw Yo-yo gimping up to the clerk supervisor's desk. Nancy Cummings walked up to Yo-yo and they engaged in conversation. She walked away shaking her head. I headed back to Ditt's route.

The office phone rang and over the loudspeaker I heard Yo-yo's voice, "Stanley Stegman 1016, Stanley Stegman 1016." I was waiting for it, but it didn't happen. Yo-yo did not say yo. I'm sure the conversation with Ms. Cummings had something to do with the lack of Yo-yo saying yo. I saw Ditt and he just finished racking the letters. He showed me how to fill out that yellow slip for the certified mail.

The flats were all pulled down in trays on the floor. He directed me to fetch the parcels, so I headed to the parcel section. This was where I encountered Suzy again. "Hi, Kevin."

"Good morning, Suzy," I replied.

She announced, "High of 86 degrees, no rain but very humid. So you MUST drink lots of fluids."

My first thought was, *If I drink lots of beer and get caught. I'll just say that Suzy told me to.* Of course, all I said was, "Thanks. Suzy."

I noticed that there were quite a bit of parcels, about 15, for Ditt's route. Suzy came really close to me and whispered, "Dittmeyer didn't take parcels all week." Mental note to self:

Lesson to learn. Some of these guys were not here to do the job. They were here to do as little as possible. I went back to the route and Ditt was pulling down the letters into trays. The cart was full of parcels, so Ditt instructed me to get the jeep and put the flats and parcels in it.

I mentioned, "It's like a week's worth of parcels. Your route seems to get a lot of parcels, Ditt."

"Luck of the draw," he said. "Oh, by the way, you need to gas up. You're running on fumes."   I started to really not like Ditt right now. I asked him how and where I do that. He told me the gas station that we used was on Main Street. He said to go to Main and make a right. About a mile down on the right was a Gulf station. He told me to just fill up the jeep and when I was done, go in and sign for it.

"Well, there's no gas so I really don't have a choice, do I?" I tried to sound as annoyed as I felt. I wanted the weasel to know that I knew he was screwing me. Ditt just shrugged. He didn't give a crap. I saw the pattern. Everybody, it seemed, was out for themselves. Like the piece from yesterday, you throw in an extra block. Don't deliver the parcels for a week. I hope I don't act the same way, petty and lazy.

Ditt warned, "Beware the red menace in the apartments." I had no idea what he was talking about; and he didn't offer any other information, so I let it go.

I went outside and put my mail on the loading dock. Floyd Lloyd was backing up and here it comes, BAM! Suzy was on the dock helping to unload a tractor-trailer that pulled up. She commented, "We really need to write a book about this place. My only concern is that nobody would believe it." I backed up the jeep and put everything in it. It was loaded with parcels. I went up the steps to the loading dock and Steve Mueller was leaving.

Steve said to me, "Where are you going? Don't leave that jeep just sitting there. There are other people that need to load up." I apologized and hustled to get my jeep out of his way. I moved the jeep to the street. I went back inside the office and felt the air-conditioning for the last time. It was funny, you didn't really feel the A/C when you're racking; but as soon as it was gone, you missed it. I punched out for the street and noticed Stegman animatedly talking to Hartman. Stanley's arms were flailing all over the place. I left and jumped into the jeep and looked for the gas gauge. Wow, the needle didn't really move. I hoped I would make it to the gas station. I proceeded to the gas station and was almost there when the jeep started sputtering. I said, "Come on, baby" as if my encouragement would help. I made it, filled the tank, then headed into the office. There was a woman in this dirty, dingy, non-air-conditioned office.

She informed me, "The clipboard is right there on that hook." She said in one word, "Whatareyanew?"

To which I responded, "Yup, day three and my first time gassing up."

She said, deliberately slower, "Find your route and put in the amount of gallons and price." I didn't know either so I had to go back to the pump to retrieve the information. As I was inputting the information on the clipboard, she mentioned, "Good luck, *Bueno Sarte.*"

So I started driving to what used to be Ditt's route. I had a full tank of gas and I felt good. I felt free, this was cool. I really enjoyed being outside. That was a perk of the Army. I was outside a lot. I didn't think that I would like being a clerk. I was at a traffic light on Main Street and a jeep was waiting for the light on the other side, facing me. The other jeep flashed his lights at me, and I saw that it was Catfish. The light turned green and we waved as we passed each other. I turned onto route 103 and noticed Mick pushing his cart. Man, can that guy move! His hair was parted in the middle; and with each step, it bounced like wings. I guess I was slowing him down the other day. I honked my horn and he saluted me. As I drove past him, I yelled out, "Yo, Mickster!" About a tenth of a mile down, Tim Waits was dropping off Mick's first relay. Again, I honked and waved.

I drove another ten minutes and stopped at a 7-Eleven to buy a Gatorade. I had a couple of hours of walking so I decided to take Suzy's advice and stay hydrated.

I arrived at my first relay, Cedar Street. I loaded my letters and flats into that raggedy mailbag from yesterday and embarked. Nothing special—12 houses up, cross the street, and 12 houses down. Of course, I ended up across from my jeep. I then drove to the beginning of the next relay on Elm Street. Again, not much to it. This, most definitely, was not skilled labor. We were mere overgrown paperboys. I finished Elm and drove to Chestnut. As I grabbed the letters and flats, I noticed there were two parcels for this loop. I also noticed a parcel for the first loop which I will drop off later. The parcels were for number 5 and 14 Chestnut. I put the parcels in the mailbag with the letters and flats. I began delivering, and at number 7 I realized I did not deliver the parcel to 5. So I went back and put the parcel in the mailbox. I then passed 7 and went straight to 9 to resume the loop. When I was heading back down the even side, I remembered to deliver the parcel to 14. I was two houses away from finishing the loop when I heard, "Woo-hoo, Mr. Mailman."

I looked up to see this lady coming down the street waving the parcel that I had just delivered. I waved and started walking towards her. "Yes, Ma'am," I said when we were close to each other.

"Mr. Mailman, you delivered this to the wrong house," as she handed me the package.

"Are you not 14 Chestnut?"

"Yes," she replied, "but this is East Chestnut. This package is clearly for North Chestnut, see the N right there before Chestnut? It happens all the time when Walt isn't on the route."

I stammered, "Walt?"

"Yes, Walt, our regular carrier," she said. "Actually, there is also a South Chestnut in Farmingburg, too. You would figure that they could come up with different names for the streets or at least use different numbers. After all, numbers are infinite. But whoever designed this system used the same numbers for all three Chestnuts. By the way, are you going to be our new carrier?"

I informed her, "Oh, no, I'm just filling in for Ditt, I mean Walt, today. I'm new, third day. Today is Walt's last day. He had to go to a medical appointment."

"Oh, we knew his retirement was soon. We just didn't know it was today. Well, if you see him, tell him Roberta from 14 East Chestnut said congratulations and we'll miss him. And good luck to you."

It was then that I took notice of Roberta. Nice looking. I replied, "Thank you and I'll most certainly tell Ditt, I mean Walt, when I see him today." I got in the jeep and finished my warm Gatorade. I debated going back to the 7-Eleven or to the deli which was closer. I decided to go back to 7-Eleven as it was cheaper, but I was going to knock out one more loop first. As I was driving to the next loop, Spruce Street, a jeep was coming down the block. It was Lamore and he pulled right up to 14 EAST Chestnut, Roberta's house. I began my loop on Spruce Street. Up one side and down the other. I got in the jeep and headed to the 7-Eleven. I turned around and Mr. Bobby Lamore was coming down the steps from 14 East Chestnut. It seemed that he avoided eye contact with me but had a huge smile on his face. The man lived up to his reputation. At this point, he became one of my heroes, too. Man, I surely needed some and decided that I was going to pursue Lucy. Got to give it a shot. As I was driving down Chestnut, I could see Roberta behind the curtains watching Lamore getting in his jeep. I made it to the 7-Eleven and purchased a Super Big Gulp and a Gatorade. I was thirsty but not hungry at all. I almost finished the super gulp and drove back to the route. I really would like to get this thing done. A couple more loops.

Next loop up was Fir Drive for which there was an extremely large parcel. I delivered the parcel before I began as it was way too large to carry with the mail. I placed the parcel on the steps and knocked, then went back to the jeep and drove to the corner. I got out of the jeep and started the loop. When I got to 13 Fir where I dropped off the package, a little old lady was at the door. I read the name on the letter and saw that her name was Emma Lagone. I greet her with, "Hello, Emma" She replied, "Thank you for dropping off that package. This is for your trouble," and she held out her hand which contained a couple of dollar bills.

I immediately said, "Thank you so much, but it was no trouble. I'm just doing my job. I just couldn't."

She replied, "Please, let me show you my appreciation." Again I told her that I couldn't possibly take it. After an Abbott and Costello routine that went on for way too long, I relented and took the money so as not to hurt her feelings. I thanked her again and told her that I would buy a cold soda. Emma added, "Or maybe a cold beer." I like the way Emma thinks.

Emma started telling me that the parcel was from her son and grandson who live in Arizona. I had noticed that the postmark was from Prescott. Emma started telling me that she was thinking of moving there. She went on about the low cost of living and the dry climate. I was standing there with more than half the loop to go. I felt bad but I had to get out of this conversation and finish this route. I told Emma that I was running late and might get in trouble. She asked me if I would come back to talk to her when I was done. She said that Walter always came back to talk and have some tea. I reminded her that I was new and still figuring things out and was really running late. Emma looked sad, but I headed down the steps and went about my business. When I was on the other side of the street, I saw Emma on the porch. She might have been trying to beckon me across, but I just waved and continued on my way and finished the loop. I drove to Maple Street and, much to my delight, it was only eight houses but three parcels. I finished quickly.

Again, to my surprise, the last part of the route were apartments. These apartments were different from the apartments on Mick's route. These apartments were only one floor. There was a mailbox outside each door. The front of the apartments had a big lawn and a swimming pool. There didn't appear to be a place to park in the front so I drove around the back. Right in the middle was an opening and the mail was racked to start there. Although I had five parcels, I figured I would deliver the mail first and then the parcels. These were the Fieldstone apartments Ditt warned about, something about the red menace. I started delivering and, man, I was making good, no great, time. The mailboxes were big and I just lifted the top and deposited mail without breaking stride. I finished the first part, 30 apartments in ten minutes. I did the other half in less than 10 minutes. I then did the parcels. Two parcels to go and I heard, "Hey melman, melman." There was a big red-headed woman walking towards me. "Are you the new melman? Wait, you don't even have a uniform. Who are you? Are you an imposter?"

"I'm just doing the route for Walt today. It's only my third day," I said to her. And who the hell would impersonate a mailman, or "melman," as she referred to us.

"Well, I'm expecting a very important letter; and Walt said the new melman would have it. You're not even a real melman, so you're not going to have it."

I was kind of lost in this conversation so I just said, "Okay, have a nice day." She walked away, to my relief. As I went back to the jeep, I saw only one person in the pool and a lifeguard. What a waste. Man, I would be poolside if I could. I would go in right now if I could. It hit me that I only had to empty the mailbox and I would be finished.

First route by myself and mission completed! I could do this, well, for the time being. After all, look at what this place did to people. It seemed everyone had issues or had what could be described as a quirk. These people were not normal. I mean, a guy like Yo-yo fit right in. I mean, a guy like Mick seemed alright, but I'm sure given time, well, who knows. But I definitely didn't want to get sucked in and do thirty years. Whoa, whoa, one task at a time. I was thinking about thirty years. I had to empty that mailbox on Lafayette first. I drove to the mailbox and there were 11 letters in it and one empty beer can. It was almost 2:00 and I had until 3:00. I finished the warm Gatorade which, I might add, was still good.

I figured that I would go to the McDonald's on Mick's route to finish out the day. I could get another soda and small fries and sit in the air-conditioning. I realized between the coffee truck, the Gatorades, and McDonald's, I spent thirty bucks. I couldn't do that every day. I still had three and a half weeks to get paid. Again, I reminded myself, one thing at a time. I began to enjoy the A/C and the time flew by. Before I knew it, I needed to drive back to the office.

I pulled in the parking lot, unloaded, and it was a totally different atmosphere. I saw Eugene and said, "What's up, Eugene?" The man looked at me like he had never seen me before.

"Hi," he said sheepishly.

Yo-yo and Mike the Mortician were sitting at the carrier supervisor desk. Hartman saw me and yelled "Yo, yo. It's my man, Kev J. I'm sorry, Mike, I know I'm not supposed to say yo, but I am getting better."

"That you are, Eric. That you are," Mike assured him. He informed me that I would be holding down Ditt's route until it was awarded to the highest bidder. Mike said that the new carrier wouldn't start until a week from Monday at the earliest. He then instructed me to go throw whatever mail was over there and get familiar with the route. I asked him if it was alright to go to the restroom first. Mike said, "Of course, please go wash up. I'm going to look into getting you guys lockers so you can keep a towel and maybe a dry shirt there. Also, it's a good place to keep your rain gear. Let me tell you, it is necessary to have good rain gear. Once you get your feet wet, it is a long day." I was starting to warm up to Mike. He seemed like a decent guy. My only problem with the guy was that he hangs out with Lucy.

 I used the bathroom and felt much better after I washed my face and hands. I went to the route and started racking bulk mail. I noticed there was a list of the names and numbers of the customers on East Chestnut. At the top, it noted that if the name was not on this list, that mail does not belong to this route. I went back to racking the mail and started utilizing advice from Eugene. When I got a letter for Chestnut, instead of stopping and looking at the list, I made a pile. I racked all of Chestnut at the same time and was starting to remember the names on East Chestnut. I noticed the last name for 14 was Pearlman. Yup, the Pearlman family—Mr. Charles Pearlman and Roberta Pearlman. Ah ha, a little extramarital activity. Oh, well, it happens. After half an hour I was done with the letters and started on the flats. My boy Eric Hartman comes by, "Yo, yo, yo, What's up, Kev? Yo, I really pulled some strings for you to get this route till the new guy gets it, yo. Plus, I'll be needing a ride home when we leave at 6:00." I was working till 6:00? That's news. I was annoyed. "You asking me or telling me, Eric? Suppose I'm busy."

 He seemed hurt. "Yo, I'm sorry Kev. You know you're my best friend. I can always get Gladys to come get me if you're busy."

 "No, I'm not, but suppose I was. I didn't want you to get stuck," I lied. I felt bad about Gladys having to come get him. And he was doing that "best friend" thing again. I wasn't even aware there was an Eric "Yo-yo" Hartman three days ago. "Alright, buddy, 6:00 we are out of here."

 Mike the Mortician approached and asked if I could help him out. He had two express mail that just came in that he needed delivered. Help him? No, thank you, Mike, for getting me out of this awkward situation. "Sure, Mike I got you on this one." I took the express mail and saw they were both for the business section of town. Think about it, in three days I was on top of this carrier thing and Yo-yo was making administrative decisions.

Mike told me that I could take any jeep in the parking lot. I got the keys to the jeep for Ditt's old route because I figured it had gas. I drove toward the business district where there were small factories, warehouses, retail stores, and small machine shops. I noticed that the traffic was heavier than earlier in the day. Hey, I was in no hurry. I got paid by the hour.

I made it to the first stop, Flaherty's Furniture Outlet and Showroom. I went through the front door and headed to the customer service desk. They directed me to a guy named Oscar in the sales department. Oscar was eager to receive the large envelope. I showed him where to sign and he let out a big "whoooo." Oscar shook my hand and then grabbed and hugged me. I was startled as he explained that he just closed a huge deal but was not sure the other party was serious about the deal. "Bro, you made my day, no, my week, okay, my month. This got here fast, I'll get the boss off my back for quite a while with this baby. Whooo!" I realized it was really cool to make someone that happy by just doing my job. I headed for the door and proceeded to the next delivery.

I MEET MY DREAM GIRL

The factory/warehouse, Four Seasons, was only a half-mile away. Between lights and traffic it took me almost fifteen minutes to get there. I walked into the lobby and there were two secretaries/receptionists that were dressed up almost as if they were going out. Plenty of make-up, nice tight dresses, and "fuck me now" high heels. One was answering the phone and the other was facing away from me making copies. It had been awhile since my last encounter, and I had to admit these two girls got my blood circulating. The girl making copies turned around and WOW!! What a doll! Smoking body, very cute. The other girl finished her phone call. The hot one said, "Remember, Janet, we're going to the Modern on Saturday night to see Morbid Obesity."

"Yes, Crispy, we're going Saturday night to see your boy, Mike Pittman. I think you have a morbid obsession."

I was just standing there and said, "Hello, I have express mail here."

Right away, the phone rang and Janet answered, "Hello, can I give you all the reasons to choose Four Seasons? Yes, I will put you through."

I turned to Crispy. "So, you're a fan of Morbid Obesity? You really don't look like a speed metal fan."

Crispy objected, "What does a speed metal fan look like? I'm more of a fan of Mike Pittman. Speed metal helps me with my workouts, I love it."

Janet chimed in, "Crispy's a badass. She kickboxes and is really good, too."

Crispy explained, "I feed off the energy of metal when I'm training, Hey, you work at the Post Office, right? Do you know Mike Pittman?"

I gave them my story about just getting out of the Army and that I only started this week at the Post Office. I said, "I've spoken with Mike, and he seems like a really nice guy."

Crispy was really excited and asked, "Can you introduce me to him?"

I responded, 'I would imagine so, but I need someone to sign for this."

The phone rang again and Janet said, "Get that, Crispy."

So I heard, "Hello, can I give you all the reasons to choose Four Seasons?"

I asked, "Crispy?" Janet explained that her name was Chrissy and her last name started with a P, something Italian. She told me that she was a little spacey, too.

As she signed, Janet continued, "She calls me Janet from another planet." She said that Chrissy was quite smitten with Pittman. I was making small talk with Janet and asked her who she had a crush on.

She responded, "Ex-military and, you know, government employees."

I could not believe my ears. So I took the bait, "Well, you're going to have to give me your number then," and she did. Wow, I was beginning to really enjoy this job. Ideally, I would rather have had Chrissy's number, but I was happy. We chatted for a couple of minutes, and I told Janet that I would call her that night. We would go to lunch soon and would definitely be going to the Modern bar to see Morbid Obesity on Saturday night where I would try to hook up Chrissy with Pittman. I said goodbye to the girls and was floating on air as I got to my jeep and headed back to the office.

It was a couple of minutes after 5:00 and the traffic was ridiculous. Halfway back to the office, I thought of Lucy and my heart dropped. I barely knew her, but I almost felt like I was cheating on her. It was funny; but suddenly, I had confidence that I did not have earlier in the week. I figured that I should make a play for Lucy when I got back to the office. It was still warm out although it was after 5:00. Also, the traffic was heavy.

Finally, I arrived back at the good old Farmingburg Post Office and parked the jeep in the lot. As I walked to the loading dock, I saw Joey Rags unloading his jeep. He asked, "Hey, new guy, how much overtime did ya get?" I explained to him that I came in at 8:30 and was getting a straight eight hours. He replied, "Straight eight, pfff, I'm getting two hours O.T. and an hour V time." I knew that anything after eight hours was time and a half, but I found out that anything after 10 hours was double time. So Joey was getting an hour of double-time, nice. Regional kept statistics on overtime and V time, and they frowned upon V time. Each office tried to keep V time to a minimum. I wondered if in the Regional reports V time was highlighted. Also, I realized that my boy Joey was a one-upper. Whatever you did or had, Joey did or had one more. If you said you had two houses Joey would go "Pfff, I have three." If you said you made $70,000 a year, Joey would say, "Pfff, I made $80,000," whether it was true or not. Well, I was eager to get inside to the comfy confines and the air-conditioning.

As I climbed the stairs, I saw a postal tractor-trailer parked at the other end of the loading dock. There was a clerk that I hadn't seen before, and he was pushing these carts of outgoing mail and parcels into the trailer. I was heading for the door, and it seemed the clerk was having trouble with the cart that he was pushing up a slight incline into the truck. As my hands were empty, I went over and gave the guy some help. With minimal effort, the cart went right into the trailer. The guy thanked me and introduced himself, "Hey, thanks. I'm Corey, THE DOCKMASTER!!" he emphasized. "This is my domain." I'm pretty sure that I smelled alcohol on his breath.

I introduced myself, " Hey, I'm Kevin Johnson. They call me J."

He replied, "What are ya, new? I've never seen you before." As he asked, I noticed there was an older guy sitting on the dock watching us. It seemed he was there the whole time.

I told Corey, "Yeah, I started Monday. It's my third day."

He showed me a pint of liquor in his pocket and said, "I started two months ago, You want a swig?"

I turned him down and said, "Definitely another time." I came down the ramp and the guy on the dock nodded to me so I nodded back.

Corey introduced me. "Hey J, this is Guy the truck driver."

I said, "What's up, Guy?"

Guy must have felt guilty when he explained, "I'm not allowed to touch the mail, Union rules." I can't help but think, *Was it against Union rules to prevent someone from getting hurt?* I found out later that the truck driver drives about 45-55 minutes from the mail processing center in Melville to Farmingburg. He would back in the truck and sit there while a clerk or clerks, like Corey, filled up the trailer with outgoing mail. After a couple of hours when the truck was full, he would then drive back to Melville and some clerks would unload the truck. Seemed like an easy job. My cousin Pauly was a high school gym teacher. He claimed the hardest part of his day was to find his whistle in the morning, and the rest was all downhill after that. It would seem to the casual observer that these had to be two of the easiest jobs there were. It made me realize that I must re-evaluate my career choices, especially if I didn't want to end up like Dittmeyer. Suddenly, Corey started yelling at somebody dropping off some of those white plastic postal tubs filled with mail.

I finally got inside to the air-conditioning and it was sweet. I saw Mike the Mortician at the carrier supervisor desk. He smiled and asked me how it went. I told him, "Not enough o's in smooth, boss. All taken care of." He thanked me and I could have gotten into one of those "No, thank you. No, thank you" conversations, but I dropped it and just commented, "My pleasure." If he only knew how awesome my little excursion was. I vowed not to call him the Mortician anymore, or at least make a valiant effort.

I went to the window, and Lucy took my breath away with her beauty and awesome smile. I told her that I had two express mail receipts; and she said, "Thank you, Kevin. How was your day?"

My first thought was, *How could she know how I hooked up with Janet?* I rationalized, of course, she didn't know. "I'm getting more familiar with the job and, even more important, familiar with the personalities of my co-workers."

"Oh, my God, that is so funny! Well, good luck with that. The job you will get the hang of really fast."

"Thanks for asking, Lucy." I was feeling really close to her so I blurted out, "Are you involved with anyone?"

"Oh, Kevin, you are so sweet. But I am really busy. I take classes at the university. Right now is the short summer semester. Monday through Thursday, three hours a night. And the professor expects you to be caught up with the material. The class started last week and only three more weeks after tonight. But to answer your question, I am involved with someone." My heart dropped. "My son, Julien. He is the love of my life."

Okay, she didn't mention a boyfriend so I said, "Well, good luck with that, study hard. I'm thinking of going back to school."

All of a sudden, Yo-yo interrupted, "Hey, Kev, I didn't see you come in. Hey, Lucy, Ms. Cummings is going to need…" I didn't hear him anymore. He was talking about things I never heard of plus, I was thinking, *I said 'STUDY HARD' to this beautiful individual. 'Study hard' was the best thing I could come up with?* It seemed so stupid. I sounded like a moron. I did notice that my man Yo-yo did not say "yo" once during the conversation. These two were engrossed in their conversation so I headed back to Ditt's old route, but for the time being it could be referred to as my route. I didn't think anyone else would call it Johnson's route, but I did like the way it sounded. I threw all the flats and did a sweep. I was going to be in good shape as far as route 19 was concerned.

It was ten minutes to 6:00 p.m. so I went to wash up. This place was dead. The window had been closed to the public since 5:00 p.m. There were very few clerks, and they were doing whatever they needed to finish up. A lot like the carriers in the morning, focused. What a stark contrast to all the energy in the morning. As I washed up, I was surprised again at how dirty my hands were.

Yo-yo came into the bathroom and went about his business. He asked me how I was doing out on the street. I filled him in on some of the escapades; and as he washed his hands, he asked me, "Kev do I say 'yo' a lot?"

I was flabbergasted. Was this a joke? So I responded, "Do you mean that you don't say 'yo' on purpose? I mean, for the last two and a half days you started and ended every sentence with 'yo.' Sometimes your whole sentence was just 'yo.' To answer your question, yes, you say 'yo' a lot!"

"Okay, okay, you're starting to sound like Cummings. She told me that I couldn't answer the phones if I didn't sound more professional. I'm trying, Kev, I guess it's my subconscious. I don't even know I'm doing it." I was starting to find a soft spot for this schnook. He really needed this job to support his growing family.

I offered, "Maybe you can wear a rubber band around your wrist and every time you say 'yo,' you snap the rubber band. It makes you think about a habit that you want to change."

Yo-yo said, "Yeah, yeah, that's what I will do. There are rubber bands everywhere."

I reassured him, "You will break that habit, buddy. You're doing better already. It's almost 6:00, let's get out of here."

"Aw, thanks Kev, you are the best, best friend."

As it was approaching 6:00 p.m., we were at the punch clock. It was just me, Yo-yo, and Joey Rags. So I asked Joey, "Hey Joe, you and Letterman are always quoting the M-41 letter carrier handbook. When do we get one?"

"You are the only one who's asked for one. I'll ask Letterman. Adios," as he hit the clock and walked out.

Yo-yo, I mean Eric, and I followed suit. As we walked across the dock and were ready to cross the street, the postal tractor-trailer passed us. The truck driver, Guy, honked and waved. So I waved back.

Eric asked, "Do you know him?"

"Not really. I met him on the loading dock today." We got to my car. As I drove to the Hartman residence, I realized that the traffic was lighter at 6:00 than it was yesterday at 5:00. I glanced at the gas gauge, and it dawned on me that I needed gas. So I pulled into a gas station/convenience store and filled up the tank. I went into the store to buy a six-pack of beer. I was afraid to ask Hartman if he wanted anything as he might give me a shopping list of items. I told Eric about meeting Janet and asked him if he was going to see Pittman's and Yates' band on Saturday night. Eric said that he didn't go out much, just watched the kids. When we were almost at the Hartman's house, I offered Eric a beer to take inside. He politely declined and said he didn't drink. I asked him "Never?"

Eric responded, " I don't like the taste."

Oh, well, I was just trying to be polite. More for me. Speaking of manners and being polite, my best friend could have offered a couple of bucks for gas. His house was completely out of my way. I didn't ask or say anything since I was pretty sure this guy was barely making ends meet as it was. We pulled up to the house and Eric asked me to come in. I declined, I wanted to get home and crack a cold one and take a shower. In that order, too. I bid my best friend a good night and he thanked me profusely. I headed home to my apartment.

Going inside, there was a note on the door. It was from my mom. She wrote that, of course, she missed me and had not gotten an update on the new job. The note stated that she made chicken cutlets and there were some in the fridge and I should stop in and say hello. It had been a crazy three days. So I headed upstairs to say hello and, more importantly, get some of mom's awesome chicken cutlets. The only thing better than her cutlets were her meatballs. I went in and she was sitting at her dining room table.

"Mom, how are you?" I gave her a kiss and headed to the fridge. I took the Tupperware with the cutlets and asked, "Did pop eat or can I have these?"

She said, "Yes, your father ate. You can have that. Just make sure I get my Tupperware back. There's enough for your lunch tomorrow."

"Of course, mom," I said, "there's a lot of food which, I assure you, will not go to waste."

"So, tell me about the job. How is it being a mailman?"

"Well, mom, the proper nomenclature is letter carrier, which is deceiving because most of the mail is junk mail."

Mom added, "And bills." I informed her about my days at the Post Office. We laughed when I told her about my co-workers and their various quirks and behaviors. She particularly liked Suzy Forecast. Mom brought me up to speed on my siblings and their kids' lives. I kissed her and told her to say hello to my pop. He was at the VFW hall hanging out with the other retired veterans, probably playing cards. Mom let me know that she was making meatballs this weekend which I didn't want to miss. Which I didn't.

I went downstairs to my basement apartment. I admired my mom and dad. They both worked hard and raised five kids. The old man was a retired corrections officer. He did 32 years and worked all the overtime he could. He was a little bit rough around the edges, but I guess that came from spending a third of your day in jail. Mom worked at the university in the library. They had this nice house paid off on Long Island and a place in Florida to be near my brother and his kids, their grandkids.

They used to rent the basement apartment out; but when I was getting discharged from the Army, they offered it to me. Which I totally appreciated. Don't get me started on security deposits and first and last month's rent. When I leave here, I hope it is to a place that I own. So I headed downstairs and took that shower. I ate the fried chicken cutlet straight out of the Tupperware. Didn't even warm it up. Man, I love my mom's cutlets; and I must admit they go great with the beer.

DAY 4: NO HUMP DAY

I was watching *Jeopardy* and the next thing that I knew it was 5:00 a.m. I didn't even see Final Jeopardy. My alarm was set for 5:30 so I tried to go back to sleep but couldn't. So I got out of bed and had a big bowl of cereal. I got dressed and realized that I must do laundry tonight. I could have mom do it, but I felt like a loser when I asked. All of a sudden, it dawned on me that I did not call Janet like I promised. I guess I could visit her at lunch. Her job wasn't far from route 19. So I drove to the office and went inside. I saw Syd Weir walking in. I said hello and Syd asked me how it was going. I told him pretty good. As we got to the door, Syd pointed at it, opened it, and said, "Let's do this, our destiny awaits."

There was a second door so I opened that for Syd. He walked through it and pointed to the right. "Time to punch in." I thought to myself, *I remember him pointing as he was about to sweep flats the other day; but seriously, does he point everywhere he goes?* When we got to the punch clock, at least half the guys pointed to Syd and said, "Syd!" There were about 15 guys waiting to punch in.

Most of the business guys started earlier, at 6:00 a.m. You could see Stegman sitting at his desk, angrily staring at some paperwork, probably the Regional reports. The punch clock at the Post Office was like a water cooler at an office. It was the place to be where workers gathered to talk about current events, TV shows, issues at work and with each other, and most importantly, gossip. Letter carriers were much more relaxed before they punched in than after. This was the calm before the rat race. They had time to catch up on each other's personal lives. Some guys talked about their spouses or kids. There was gossip galore, who was doing who, real and imagined. Sports talk and some inane chatter like:

Yates: Hey Pitt, you know the commercial with the camel that's talking about hump day?

Pittman: Yeah, I've seen it.

Yates: Well, we have no hump day because we work Saturdays. I mean it's Thursday already and, right now, we are only halfway through our workweek.

Pittman: So Yates, you've been here for seven years and you finally noticed we have a six-day work week?

Yates: I'm just saying we don't have a hump day.

Chooch: Yeah, no hump day. It is what it is.

But today there was a buzz going around that everyone was concerned about. It seemed that management was going to write up Del Greco for being off his appointed rounds the day he alerted the grandma on the second floor of the burning house. Del Greco was all the way on the other side of town when he did his heroic deed. According to the M-41 carrier handbook, when delivering mail, carriers were required to proceed directly to their route and begin their appointed rounds. At lunchtime, carriers were required to choose between three previously-designated lunch stops within close proximity to the route. The carrier could go to any of the three lunch stops but only those three. The carrier was then to finish the route and go back to the office. Any deviation was grounds to be written up. Of course, there were some exceptions, like going to the gas station to gas up your jeep or doing a piece on another route for overtime.

Apparently, Del Greco wasn't doing anything else; and the incident happened all the way across town. The guys were angry because management was all too happy when there was good publicity. They didn't bring this issue up when the Mayor of Farmingburg was praising Del Greco; and now when the publicity died down, they wanted to stick the knife in his back. There was a feeling of carriers versus management. Someone commented, "What are we supposed to do, not help people in an emergency?"

I saw Joey Rags, Letterman, and Stegman by the carrier supervisor desk. Joey Rags approached us and said, "Don't get too excited about it, guys. The Union is all over this. Letterman put in a call to the Union HQ. This is just preliminary. Pfff, you'll see."

Suzy Forecast walked by and said, "We really need to write a book about this. Nobody would believe it."

"Yeah, Suzy, stranger than fiction" and "They are always out to screw us," were some of the comments random people made.

Of course, the statement "It is what it is" was not anonymous. Next thing you knew, the clock struck 6:30 and it was all business. The carriers again seemed possessed and punched in and then headed straight to their routes. Del Greco's problem had been put to rest for the time being. I got to route 19 and followed suit and began racking letters. I was getting very familiar with this route. It was getting easier to rack. I knew from walking the route relatively where the letter went in the case or if it even belonged to this route. Newbies spent a lot of time looking for cubby holes on the case that were not even on the route.

After ten minutes or so, I heard my first "P. Ennis and family, we have a letter for the penis family" from my man Theo next door on route 37. I had to admit I found it charming, but I was a twisted individual. I wondered if it was a big penis family or a small penis family. Maybe I'll ask Theo later. So the Cummings contention that Theo did the penis thing only when she walked by was proven false. Apparently, he did it whenever he racked a piece of mail for the Ennis family. I was getting so much better racking this route, although I rocked right and left when I threw a letter. I was racking a tray of mail, two feet of letters, in about 25 minutes. That was pretty good, considering it was only my fourth day.

And then it happened. All of a sudden, carriers were coming by to check out route 19. Today was the first day that Ditt's old route had been posted and up for bid. Again, if a route was open, it was put up for bid and the bidder with the most seniority was awarded the route. There was a parade of potential bidders. The first was Benjy Steckel. I was racking mail and really focused on the route when I sensed a presence. I turned around and found Benjy standing behind me. He was looking over my shoulder at the route. Not knowing what was going on, I asked him, "Can I help you?"

Benjy informed me that he was considering bidding on route 19. He muttered to himself, *All residential.* The loops were not too big. He stopped thinking aloud and informed me, "I don't think that I'll be bidding on this route. The loops are a little too big for me. It's not that they are really big, but I had a hernia operation a couple of months ago. I have to be really careful how much I carry. The surgery was virtually non-invasive, but I have a scar in my belly button. Here I'll show you." He proceeded to pull his shirt out of his pants and started to unbutton all the while he was explaining "The doctor did a great job. He..."

Quentin Roosevelt appeared around the flat case just in time. "Steckel, put your clothes back on. We all know you had surgery last year. You don't need to convince the new guy. He would take your word for it. Do you doubt him, J? See Benjy, everybody believes you."

Benjy defended himself, "The doctor did such good work. I just wanted him to see. Well, I'm not going to bid this route anyway." I don't know why Steckel needed to explain to me whether or not he was going to bid on the route. I didn't have a vested interest in this route. It was no skin off my back.

Although that was not the first time I'd encountered someone who has had surgery, and while explaining their ordeal they showed the surgery scar. Once as a teenager, my friend's grandmother had some kind of surgery. She pulled her shirt to the side, and we saw way too much. That memory has scarred me to this day. While I'm sure her scar has diminished since, I can vividly remember that scene decades later.

Quentin was looking over the case. "Oh yeah, I did this route a couple of years ago. Not gonna bid on it. You have a good day, J. Can I give you a word of advice? If anyone else starts to undress in front of you, send them to Cummings' office."

We laughed, I said, "Will do, Q." Quentin Roosevelt seemed like a nice guy, although somewhat scary looking. He was about 6 foot 5 inches tall, at least 275 pounds, dreadlocks, and a beard. I understand his brother played professional football. I found out later that Q played semi-pro football. This was the kind of guy you wanted on your side in a bar fight.

I went back to racking mail, and about ten minutes later Yates appeared. He said, "Take care of my new route. I've been asking around, and nobody senior to me seems interested. Let me ask you, do you like this route?"

"I really don't have a point of reference. But I do like this route."

Yates asked me, "Did Ditt mention how much he pulls in at Christmas? I should have asked him before he left, damn. Hey, you know my band is playing Saturday night at the Modern bar down the road. You should come."

I suddenly remembered about Janet and Chrissy. So I explained to Yates, "I was delivering express mail to the Four Seasons Showroom yesterday. There were two girls there. One of them is a big fan of the band."

Yates commented, "Only one of them?" We both laughed.

I mentioned to him, "The one has it real bad for Pittman."

Yates responded, "That don't narrow it down at all. The ladies love the Pitt-man. The ladies are crazy for him. He could seriously rival Lamore if he wanted to."

"I'm planning on being there with these girls. I'm kinda hitting on the other one. It might help me out if I could introduce them to you."

"You take care of my route and you get your intro," and he turned to leave.

I yelled out, "Thanks," and it dawned on me that I didn't know his first name.

As he was leaving, George the Bird strutted over. "Hey, just looking" Less than a minute later he just turned and walked away.

Right away, Syd Weir came over and pointed at the route and asked, "Is this the route that's up for bid?"

"Yes, it is," I replied.

Syd commented, "It's not a bad route. I did it when I was a part-timer years ago when Ditt had surgery on his foot. I liked it and I'm going to bid, but Yates is going to squeeze me out. We came in on the same day, but he is considered ahead of me. It looks like it's his if he wants it." Syd pointed away from the case and walked away. I began to wonder if these people had these quirks in their behavior or did this place do it to them.

My thoughts were interrupted by the words, "BREAK TIME!" I headed for the door and the coffee truck which was also affectionately known as the roach coach. I ran into my man Roddy, "Hey, bud, how you been? I didn't see you at all yesterday."

"Hey, Kevin. Yes, Stanley put me on an auxiliary route, I like it."

We headed to the food truck and the food truck guy commented, "Hey, look at you guys. You don't look as lost as you did on Monday." We both got coffee and a bagel. A car came speeding down the street and pulled up across the street. The coffee truck was packing up as Eric got out of the car. I could see

Gladys driving. She waved and rolled her eyes at the same time. I could feel her pain as I waved back.

The truck was leaving as Hartman limped across the street. He yelled, "Kev, get me a soda and a doughnut!" as he hobbled into the office. The truck pulled away and there was no way I could honor his request.

I glanced at my watch. It was 8:38. I assumed Eric was supposed to be at work at 8:30. Roddy and I headed into the office and sat in front of his route. At break time, the carriers would break off into their cliques. They sat at certain routes. Some guys went to the break/coffee room. Others went to their cars. There was a deli within a two-minute walk, and some even drove to the 7-Eleven around the block. Roddy told me about the auxiliary route. It was strictly businesses and only six hours, between racking and delivering. Roddy confided that he had to take his mom to dialysis twice a week. This route was perfect, so he could leave early on Tuesday and Friday. The route began at 6:00 a.m. like most of the other business routes. On the days he didn't take his mom for her appointments, Stegman had pieces of other routes for him to deliver. Roddy then asked me how I was doing. I told him that I was holding down route 19 until the highest bidder was awarded the route. Then I told him about delivering the express mail to Four Seasons and meeting Janet and Chrissy.

He commented, "You sly dog! Which one are you interested in? Is her friend available?" I told him how Chrissy loved Pittman and Yates' band, Morbid Obesity, and how she had a thing for Pittman. "Oh, she's a groupie."

In defense, I said, "I wouldn't say 'groupie.' Chrissy is a kickboxer and likes to workout to speed metal. Who just so happens to have a keen interest in the singer."

"That's a groupie, my friend. I would be very careful if I were you." My first thought was, *You are not me and why does he want to rain on my parade?*

I then brought up the fact that I told Janet that I was going to call last night but forgot. Roddy suggested that I buy a small floral arrangement for her desk, not a single rose, but a small arrangement in a vase. For the rest of the day, people would comment on her flowers and that would make me look good. He told me there was a florist at the other end of Main Street.

As I was considering Roddy's advice, Eric showed up and asked, "Yo, Kev, did you get my soda and doughnut?" I had to disappoint him and tell him the truck was pulling away when he asked.

I then called him out, "Did I hear you say 'yo?'"

"Dang, I'm really hungry. You should have stopped him, Kev. And I didn't say yo."

I lied when I said, "I tried to stop him, Eric. He wouldn't stop, and you did say yo."

Somebody yelled "BREAK OVER!" He asked to borrow money and Roddy gave him $5.

Eric informed us, "I'm going to the deli, but I don't know what I can get for $5. Thanks, Roddy. You're a good guy."

Roddy turned to rack as I headed to route 19 thinking, *Maybe Roddy and Hartman can be besties, and I can be off the hook as Eric's newly acquired best friend.* As I went past the parcel section, Stegman was still on the phone. The baseball hat was going back and forth. It really was a sight to see. As I walked past, I mimicked what I experienced the other day and yelled out, "It's alive." I went to my route, well route 19, and started racking. In a couple of minutes I was out of letters and flats.

I went to sweep early and saw Flacco and Gordon engaged in a conversation. They spotted me and Flacco yelled, "Here comes the FNG carrier." From my military experience, I knew FNG meant the Fucking New Guy. I stared them down and just said, "Waz up, fellas," like I was annoyed.

They were quiet as I moved to the next case and ran into a guy I'd never seen. He introduced himself, "Hello, I'm John Keppler. This letter is for East Chestnut, although it is addressed to North Chestnut." He handed me the letter and there were some things written on the front by the address. Somebody wrote n/7 and n/13. These routes both had a Chestnut Street on them. Route 7 had North Chestnut and route 13 had South Chestnut. The letter was addressed to North Chestnut, but it was actually for East Chestnut. This letter was being kicked back and forth between route 7 and route 13. There was also some writing on the letter. *This is the third time route 13 got this letter. n/13 means this letter does not go to route 13.* Underneath that somebody wrote, *I don't care.* Keppler said to me, "Expedite this expeditiously to East Chestnut, Thank you very much." I looked at all the penmanship on this letter and wondered who would do something like this. Then the two jackals, Gordon and Flacco, started yelping about something; and it dawned on me, *These two, that's who.*

Keppler commented, "I see you're wearing a Neal Young shirt. Are you a fan?" I said that I was and that I had seen him in concert three times. Keppler continued, "I love Mr. Young, I hope he tours again soon."

I responded, "Nice meeting you."

I was contemplating how postal workers could be so callous to their job as I headed to Stegman so he could count my mail. He motioned for me to come over to him. I was almost next to him when he looked up and yelled, "It's alive!" Oh shoot, he knew it was me.

I defended myself by saying, "Just trying to have some fun here, Stan."

"Yeah, we are all about having fun here at Farmingburg. Remember, Johnson, I hold grudges." Busted, I headed back to route 19. Stan then yelled, "23-5 sweep. Guys from the first aisle go to sweep."

Suzy Forecast was by the parcel section offering, "60 percent chance of rain today. Bring your rain gear with you. Even if it does not rain, you can always bring it back. If it rains, it's going to rain cats and dogs. And remember, even when it rains you still need to hydrate."

Somebody yelled out, "Thanks, Suzy" and "She's right. When your shoes get soaked, the rest of your day sucks even more."

I was finished with all my mail and flats and was about to pull down when the lovely Lucy came by with the accountables. I was intoxicated by her beauty and asked her if she was wearing Coco Chanel. She told me that she was. I adored everything about this woman. She had three certified letters and my keys for the box on Lafayette. I was sitting down writing those yellow slips for the certified mail. Stanley came by and asked me how much over I was going to be. I told him a half-hour, and he informed me that I would be walking a piece on Theo's route, route 37. Stan didn't ask, he just said, "You do whatever he is over today. He is having an eight-hour day."

I extended an olive branch and said, "You got it, boss. By the way, I apologize about that wisecrack."

Stan replied, "Huh…. oh, yeah, that. Whatever." Maybe he had a lot on his mind, but it didn't appear that he held grudges as long as he thought he did.

I finished pulling down my route and stacking my trays then went over to Theo's route right next door. I was happy to get as much overtime as possible. "Theo, I'm getting a piece on your route."

He informs me that it was going to be at least an hour until he would be ready to pull down. He suggested that I do my route and then come back to the office to pick up the piece. His route was the other way, west side of town, and I would pretty much have to pass the office to do his route.

I couldn't help myself when I asked, "Do I get to deliver to the Penis family? I have to ask, is it a big penis family?" Theo did not say anything, but he shook his head no. I added, "No, a small penis family would be good because I don't want to deliver to a big penis family. It might make me feel insecure." I looked at Theo and expected him to laugh, but he just kept shaking his head no.

All of a sudden I heard, "PTF Johnson, that kind of language will not be tolerated in this office. Is that understood?" Stegman! Now I knew why Theo was acting the way he did. Busted, Superintendent Cummings was standing right behind him. I offered Ms. Cummings my apology.

At this point, my interaction with Cummings was the prime attraction in the Farmingburg Post Office. Both carriers and clerks were curious as to what was transpiring.

Stegman came over and insisted, "I'll take care of it, Ms. Cummings," as she steamed away.

"Well, well, Johnson. That's two times in the past hour your big mouth has put your ass in an unfavorable light. Is this a sign of things to come? Expect to be written up at the very least. Do you think that you can go the rest of the morning without screwing up?"

I responded, "Yes sir, Mr. Stegman, my apologies."

Stan replied, "That's apology number 2, and please do not do not call me sir."

I felt like a complete ass. I recalled Letterman saying that the walls had ears. I think, in my case, it was more of bad timing. Oh, well, can't change the past. But I needed to be more careful.

Roddy came by and asked if I was okay. "The guys are saying you called Cummings a bitch." I told him that was not true and filled him in on what happened.

Carriers walked past and one commented "Way to go, Johnson. Don't take that B.S. from her." I didn't know how or why this thing got so distorted, but I wasn't objecting. I had my route pulled down so I headed to the parcel section, Three parcels today. Then I headed to the bathroom to wash up. As I approached, there were guys coming out gagging.

I knew what that meant, Flacco is or was there. He took pride in stinking out the place. I took a deep breath and washed my hands. Man, I hoped the stench didn't permeate into my clothes. I got out fast.

As I was walking away from the bathroom, I saw Gordon the

clerk. "Way to stand up to Cummings. Nobody likes her. You have to assert yourself." Again, I just stared at him and nodded my head. I didn't like him or his pal, Stinky Flacco.

I saw Syd heading for the bathroom and warned him, "Hey, Flacco was just in there. Be careful!"

Syd turned around and pointed in the opposite direction and said, "I'm going to pass then. I'll just tie it in a knot. I'll go after I load my jeep. Thanks for the heads up, I appreciate it."

I put all my mail on a skid and headed out. I backed my jeep to the loading dock, put the mail in the jeep, then moved it so other guys could load up. I then headed back in to punch out for the road. Roddy saw me and asked for my empty skid. I said, "Of course, buddy."

It was warm and sunny as I pulled out of the parking lot. I drove down Main Street and stopped at the florist. There was a small vase with some really nice flowers in it for twelve dollars. I was completely satisfied with my purchase. Nice enough but not too extravagant. I didn't want to look as desperate as I was. I proceeded to route 19 and began delivering the mail. It was a good day. The weather was great, and I was making good time. I knocked out a couple of loops. As I began the loop at East Chestnut, I noticed that it had gotten very cloudy. Halfway through, it started to drizzle. I didn't have a raincoat or any rain gear, for that matter. I walked quickly across the grass and got back to the jeep as the skies opened up and it started pouring. It was just like Suzy said, only I would have to change 60 percent to 100 percent.

It was 11:30 so I figured that I could take lunch and go see Janet. I was a little nervous and hoped she was understanding. It was around a ten-minute drive, and "I can give you all the right reasons to choose Four Seasons" kept popping into my head. It was raining hard as I ran to the lobby. Janet was on the phone and didn't see me at first. Chrissy shot me a death stare. Obviously, she knew that I didn't call last night. When she saw the flowers she seemed to soften up a little.

"Look who it is, 'Mr. I Promise to Call and Doesn't.'" Menacingly, Chrissy stated, "You don't want to mess with my friend."

Janet hung up and said coldly, "Hey, how are you? Look, you're all wet. I prayed for that rain. Now I feel bad. Where's your raincoat? Who are those flowers for? Me?" She was acting so coy, which she looked cute doing.

"Of course, the flowers are for you." I explained to her that I'd had dinner with my mom because I hadn't seen her since I started the job. I told her that we talked so much and when I finally went downstairs, I immediately fell asleep and didn't wake up until 5:00 a.m. "I didn't think that was a good time to call."

She agreed, "You are so right. Don't ever, ever, ever call me at 5:00 a.m." We laughed.

The phone rang and Chrissy answered, "I can give you the reasons to choose Four Seasons."

I said to Janet, "I am so looking forward to Saturday night. When I call tonight, we can discuss plans. Oh, by the way, I spoke with Yates, the bass player in Morbid Obesity. He assured me that I can get both of you an introduction."

Janet said, "Tell Chrissy when she gets off the phone. I'm not interested in those guys. My interest lies elsewhere." As she said this, she looked me straight in the eyes and smiled. I thought, *Wow, my slump just might be over.* A door opened in the lobby and a guy in a suit came out. He informed Janet that he was stepping out for lunch.

Janet said, "Of course, Mr. Ford. Have a nice lunch."

Mr. Ford looked me up and down and noticed the mail truck outside. "Is the mail here already?"

"Oh no, Mr. Ford. This is my friend, Kevin. He stopped by to give me these nice flowers. Aren't they beautiful?"

Ford said, "Nice little bouquet. I wish he would have brought the mail." I looked outside and it was raining really hard. There were puddles in the street; and to think, it was a gorgeous day less than an hour and a half ago. Janet gave me a hug and told me she was looking forward to Saturday night, too.

Chrissy was still on the phone and made a sign across her throat and mouthed, "Remember, I will kill you." It was kind of cute that she was concerned about her friend. I didn't think she could kill me; but I had to admit, I didn't want to find out.

I ran out to my jeep and got soaked in the process. As I drove to route 19, the rain slowed down. I pulled up to Fir Street and started the loop. When I got to Emma Lagone's house, she was waiting at the door. "Come in, come in. Do you want some tea, Kenny? Where is your raincoat?"

I corrected her, "It's Kevin. I know I should have a raincoat, but I didn't expect this. It was so nice an hour ago. I am going to get a raincoat real soon."

Emma looked me up and down. "You're about the same size as my late husband, Carmine. I'm sure his raincoat will fit you." She gave me a cup of tea and disappeared. After five minutes she showed up with a navy blue overcoat and a pair of rubbers for my shoes. "I'm so happy I found these galoshes, and this coat should fit you." The raincoat had a slight mothball smell, but it fit like a glove. The rubbers went right over my wet sneakers. The wet shoes were heavy, but at least they wouldn't get worse. I finished my tea and thanked and hugged Emma.

She said, "Kenny, I want you to have these. I'm so glad they fit. I just ask that you come to visit me every now and then." I promised that I would and I meant it. I told Emma that I was a little behind schedule and had to go. She asked, "Have you heard from Walt, Kenny?"

Again, I tried to correct her, "It's Kevin, and today is Dittmeyer's first full day of retirement. No we haven't heard from him."

She responded, "Wow, it seems longer than that. Stay dry, Kenny." I left and restarted the loop. When I was across from Emma's house, I noticed that she was standing in the doorway. I waved and she waved back. I'm so grateful for this sweet lady, and the raingear she gave me made a big difference.

When the grass is wet, your uncovered shoes get even wetter. The mail gets wet, too. The bundle of letters in my hand was exposed to the rain, and the letters at the end of the loop got it the worst. The flats made out better because they were in the mailbag. I was making good time. I thought subconsciously, I was walking faster because of the rain. The rain slowed down considerably, but it was a little more than a constant drizzle. I realized that I must pay better attention to Suzy Forecast's weather reports. Apparently, they were accurate.

The rain started pouring again as I finished the apartments. All I had to do was empty the mailbox on Lafayette. As I was bent over getting that white plastic postal bin out of the mailbox, a horn honked and I could see a female in the car. She was waving a letter and apparently wanted me to come and get her letter. There was one letter in the back of the mailbox that escaped the white bin. As I was reaching for the renegade letter, she honked again. I held up my index finger to indicate that I was busy and would get her letter shortly. How annoying! Was I supposed to jump because she had a letter to mail? I closed the box and put the outgoing mail in the jeep. I walked over to her car and saw that it was a girl in her early twenties. She said, "I'm in a rush and didn't want to get wet; and I really, really need to mail this letter today."

I responded, "I'm in a rush, too; and I didn't want to get wet, either."

She replied, "Well, that's your job."

I'm sure I could stay here for hours arguing with this girl, but I'm also sure her thinking wouldn't change. She did say, "Thank you very much." I told her to have a nice day. She drove off and I was happy that I finished route 19.

I drove back to the office because I needed to get that piece on Theo's route. When I got inside, I saw two trays of mail on the shelf of his route. Mike was sitting at the carrier supervisor's desk. He put down the phone and asked, "Johnson, are you available to do this piece on route 44?"

I let him know that I had the piece on route 37. He said that would cause me to go over ten hours, resulting in V time, which was double time. He told me he would get somebody else to do the piece. Although I wouldn't be opposed to some V time, I did just walk a route and now I had to walk some more, at least an hour. I grabbed the two trays and there was a note that the piece was an hour and twenty minutes. I glanced at the clock. It was 2:35, plenty of time to do this route and be back by 5:00. I headed out the door and I saw Floyd Lloyd backing up to the dock. I paused because I had to see if he crashed every time he backed up.

Floyd was like, "Oh baby, oh baby, I got it" and BAM, right into the loading dock.

Cody was doing his thing on the dock and I said, "Dock master! What's up, Cody?"

Cody looked at me and said, "Do I know you?"

I could smell the alcohol. He was past buzzed and I was sorry I said anything. I informed him, "I met you yesterday."

Cody mumbled, "Oh yeah, oh yeah. Do you need something? Do you want a swig?" as he showed me the bottle.

"Nah, I'm good, but thanks for the offer."

I put the two trays in the truck and headed off to route 37. The rain had slowed down significantly. I stopped at the 7-Eleven and noticed a jeep outside. At the door, Eugene was coming out. "Hey Kevin, how's it going?" he asked. Man, this guy was hot and cold. Maybe he was bipolar.

"What's up, Eugene?" I mentioned that I was holding down Ditt's old route and that it was going well.

He told me that his wife Johanna asked about my interest in being employed by the Long Island Rail Road and that I needed to be persistent. He said he was heading back to the office and I mentioned that I was on my way to route 37.

He left as I headed in for a Big Gulp. I decided that I wanted a Super Gulp instead. It was bigger and I was really thirsty. As I was filling my cup, I saw the Double Gulp. If they made a bigger soda cup, I imagined they would have to attach it to your back like a knapsack and have the straw come around from the back. I realized that I had to concentrate on more important things.

I got to the route and realized there were only three loops. But as I drove down to the first loop, it was quite a drive. I was halfway down Pinehurst Drive where the first loop began. There was at least half a foot of flats and three bundles of letters. This was the biggest loop I had done so far. At least the rain had stopped for the time being. At the fifth house, I could feel the weight of the mail digging into my shoulder. At the tenth house, number 22, a lady was waiting. She said, "I see you are walking on everybody's lawn. That is so rude. You're not going to walk on my lawn. My mother is across the street at 25 Pinehurst. You will not walk across her lawn either, understood?" I handed her the mail as she continued, "You don't appear to be too smart. Is that why are you so late?"

I replied, "It's only my fourth day, and I already walked a route."

"Theo is always here by 11:30."

I stated the obvious, "Well, Theo isn't here today" as I walked away.

She called after me, "I should call your supervisor and get you in trouble."

I called back, "If that makes you happy, be my guest."

"Okay, Mr. Wiseguy, I will."

I finished going down the evens and headed up the odds. I hoped that it didn't start raining again. I got to 25 and I forgot, accidentally walking on the lawn. The lady came flying out of her house screaming at me. I told her that I forgot and that I was sorry. She was cursing me out as I kept walking. I finished the loop and was delivering the other half of Pinehurst when Mrs. Silverstein called the Post Office.

Hartman answered the phone, "Farmingburg Post Office, how may I help you?"

"This is Amy Silverstein. I live at 22 Pinehurst Drive." She explained the situation and Eric told her that he would direct her call to a carrier supervisor.

Eric said over the loudspeaker, "Carrier supervisor 1016, carrier supervisor 1016." Stanley Stegman was long gone and Mike was outside in the parking lot where Steve Graves was showing him a problem with his jeep. Eric announced again, "Carrier supervisor 1016, carrier supervisor 1016" over the loudspeaker.

Pittman, Mueller, and Joey Ramonski were at the punch clock waiting to punch out. They looked at each other and Pittman asked, "So who wants to be the carrier supervisor?"

Joey Ramonski said, "Hey ho, I'll do it." He went to the desk and picked up the phone. "Hello, Stanislaus Hansen here, carrier supervisor of Farmingburg Post Office. How can I be of assistance?"

The guys at the punch clock howled with laughter.

Joey Ramonski continued, "Yes, what did the carrier do?...He walked across your lawn .....and your mother's lawn, too, across the street.... AFTER you told him not to....I see and he was a real...pardon me....a real weisenheimer....What exactly did he say so I can put it in my report...So it was more his attitude than what he said...Yes ma'am, yes ma'am, and your mail was late..... Yes, yes, what time are you supposed to get your mail?....by 11:00 a.m...Yes, ma'am. I will personally look into this matter myself. Yes, ma'am, Stanislaus Hansen, I assure you I will handle this matter personally. Goodbye, ma'am."

The guys were laughing so hard. Joey said, "It was so hard for me not to laugh, I almost blew it."

Apparently, this was something the carriers liked to do later in the afternoon when a supervisor was not around. I finished the piece on route 37 and a car pulled up to me. It was

DAY 4: NO HUMP DAY | 123

Silverstein, "I called your supervisor. You are screwed, you piece of shit,"

All I said was, "Thank you very much." Now, I was totally unaware of what had transpired, the phone call that Joey answered a couple of minutes before. But I was not too concerned as I didn't do anything to get in too much trouble. So I headed back to the office. As I went up to the loading dock, I waved to Guy the truck driver. Cody came out the swinging doors, and he was staggering. It was right about 4:30 and there were ten carriers waiting to punch out. When 4:30 came around, you didn't want to be in these guys' way.

I headed over to route 19 and there was bulk mail on the ledge. Having some time to kill, I started throwing letters. After five minutes Joey Rags came by and asked, "Pfff, what are you doing?" I informed him that I was getting a headstart on the next day. He said, "Not allowed. You rack mail when it's time to rack mail. Otherwise, we could have some kissasses racking off the clock, ya know what I mean?"

I thought that was a little strange, but I put the letters down and told him, "Never again, Joey, I promise you." So I sat down and took off my galoshes. My sneakers were pretty wet. Bruce J. Thompkins walked by and offered advice. "When you get home tonight, put newspaper in your shoes. It dries them. Looks like you're going to have to do it a couple of times tonight. Otherwise, your shoes will be damp tomorrow and that's a lousy way to start your day." I thanked him and thought of sweet Emma and how lucky I was that she was so caring. It was then that I recalled that I must call Janet tonight. To be honest, I really wanted to talk to her.

I went to turn in my accountables and keys. I was looking forward to seeing Lucy but found out that she went home early, something to do with school and the class she was taking. I admired Lucy as well as lusted after her. A different clerk, Rob, was working the window. He was a huge music guy, and he asked me if I was going on Saturday to see Morbid Obesity. I told him that I had plans to go. He said, "They are really good. I came up with the name and co-wrote a song with them."

"Cool," was all I could say. I thought about how he treated the customers and how, in turn, some customers treated us. Interesting.

I went to the bathroom and washed up. Thank goodness Flacco was not around. I headed to the punch clock. Syd pointed at me and asked, "Didja get a deuce?" I shook my head that I didn't understand. So he repeated, "A deuce, a deuce, two hours overtime."

"Oh, yeah, I picked up a piece on route 37."

Syd mentioned that Mike had a piece when he came back and he took half of it because he was an hour and a half on his own.

Joey Rags bragged to us, "Pfff, I got a deuce on my own route. They're lucky I didn't hit them for V time."

Syd pointed out, "Joey, you kill them." To which Joey just smiled.

The clock struck 5:00 p.m. and away we went. I got through the first set of swinging doors and heard, "Kev, Kev can you give me a ride at 6:00?"

I told Eric, "Not tonight, pal. I have to do laundry. Sorry." Yes, he expected me to wait an hour and then drive him a half hour the other way, wow.

"Alright, I'll have to call Gladys. She is not going to be happy," Eric informed me. I plowed through the second swinging door to freedom.

When I got home, the first thing I did was put my clothes in the washer. I then took off my shoes and put newspaper in them. I went upstairs and gave mom a kiss and said hi. She let me know that meatloaf was on the menu, my dad's favorite. I took a piece with some string beans. At 6:00, I called Janet. She was extremely concerned how I made out in the rain and how my day was. We talked effortlessly for 45 minutes. I told her that I was going to finish my laundry and would call back. I checked my shoes and took the wet newspaper out and replaced it with dry newspaper. I threw my clothes in the dryer and put on *Jeopardy*. After that, I got my clothes and folded them while I was watching *Wheel of Fortune*. I checked my shoes and the newspaper was less damp than the first time and I put dry paper in. I called Janet again and we talked until 10:00 p.m. I started to yawn and she said, "Go to sleep, baby." So we said goodnight and I washed my dinner dishes. When I laid down, I didn't pray in a traditional way. I just reflected on the day and said, "Thanks, God." Which I do.

THANK GOD IT'S...NO BIG DEAL. IT'S FRIDAY

The alarm clock sounded at 5:30. Wow, the nights were flying by. I definitely could have used another hour of shut-eye. One consolation was that it was Friday. Bad news, we work Saturday and I personally had to work on Sunday. No hump day! Tomorrow was my big date with Janet. I had cereal and got ready for work.

The atmosphere was lighter at the punch clock than usual. First of all, it was Friday, but I also found out that the guys get paid today. The pay period ends today and the new pay period starts tomorrow. In two weeks we will get paid for the last two weeks. For those of us that started this week, we will get this week's pay plus any overtime. I was anticipating getting a regular paycheck in the future. While starting postal pay isn't extravagant, it was more than military pay. I heard about a pool that the guys had where they each put in five dollars and the serial number on their pay stub was equivalent to a poker hand. Ones were aces, zeros were tens, and all the typical poker hands apply. Straight, three of a kind, full house, and so forth. It created quite a buzz; and from what I heard, MacGregor was in the lead with a straight.

Then there was the usual male-dominated schoolyard banter.

Del Greco asked no one in particular, "Just because a girl is in a porno movie, does that make her a porn star?"

Steve Graves chimed in, "I don't think acting is such a noble art form. We all do it. We get pulled over by the police—acting. We get in trouble with the wife—acting."

Joey Rags added, "Eugene tried to convince Stan that he was two hours late the other day. Academy award performance."

I then noticed Dotty and Maybel standing a few feet away from the crowd talking between themselves. I was sure they were aware of the inane conversation but were smart enough to keep their distance.

The clock hit 6:30 and all the nonsense stopped. Carriers punched in and headed to their routes, except for Del Greco. He blurted out, "All that talk about porno has me worked up. I'm going to do a selfie," as he headed to the bathroom.

I walked past Eugene and he was praying to the postal gods. Then, I saw Maybel next door on route 37. I asked her, "Is Theo in today?"

"No," she responded, "I'm his floater. He's off the weekend. Theo won't come in on his day off." I mentioned that I did a piece yesterday, Pinehurst and Bryer Drive. I mentioned that Pinehurst was the biggest loop I had ever done. Maybel interrupted, "Theo didn't break it down. Here, if you ever do Pinehurst again, make sure he breaks it down. If you look at the case on Pinehurst, there are red lines where the loop splits." I could see the smaller loops. Then I brought up number 22, Amy Silverstein. Maybel asked me what time I did the piece. I told her around three o'clock.

"Oh, boy, I'm sure she gave you an earful."

"Yes, she did. I also walked across her lawn and was scolded and warned not to walk across her mom's lawn. I completely forgot, and she was waiting for me. She actually chased me over to Breyer to curse me out."

Maybel informed me that Silverstein had been written up before for abusive language towards carriers and that I should report the incident to Stan. I just wanted to keep it "LP," like the guys say—Low Profile.

So I was racking mail and heard somebody yell, "Annie, the bag lady is here." I just kept racking and I was doing pretty good, faster still, every tray. Then I heard, "And who is this hunk of a carrier?" I turned around and met Annie for the first time. She was an official independent postal uniform distributor. After 90 days and every year thereafter, carriers get a uniform allowance. Annie had a tape measure out and wanted to measure me. I reluctantly declined but asked her about postal t-shirts. She said, "Your friend Roddy let me measure him. But the t-shirts are 15 dollars or two for twenty-five. I'll tell you what, I'll give you two for twenty."

"Deal. Do you have extra-large?"

Annie replied, "Of course I do, honey. Hey, Maybel, tell my new friend that I am the best deal in town."

Maybel came around the case. "Well, I get all my stuff from Annie. I love her." That made me feel better about doing business with Annie. I assured her that when the time came, we would make a deal. The t-shirts were not official, but they made me look more legit. Annie showed me some hooded sweatshirts that I liked, but I told Annie that I wasn't getting paid for another two weeks and it was really not the season for hoodies. I thanked her for the discount on the t-shirts and assured her we would do business down the road. She then went to chit chat with Maybel.

Almost as if he was waiting for Annie to leave, Stegman came over and told me that I would be delivering an hour and a half on route 44. Because it was a business piece, it would have to be done first. Stan also said that I would have to leave the bulk mail because I couldn't be more than a half-hour late and that I could clean the route up tomorrow. "Whatever you want, boss," I said.

Somebody yelled, "Breaktime!" and I saw my man, Roddy. We headed to the roach coach and grabbed a snack. I didn't see

Eric and was thinking of him as the coffee truck pulled away, but there was no sign of him. We headed in through the swinging doors and Gordon and Flacco were on our side sweeping our kickbacks. Stan was wearing his hat and doing his thing and these morons were taking advantage.

Gordon, who was six foot six, commented, "Doesn't the Post Office have a height requirement? I heard Lil Stan the carrier couldn't reach half of the mailboxes on his route so they made him a supervisor."

Flacco added, "Maybe he has a thyroid condition."

Del Greco walked past, "I heard excessive autoerotica can stunt your growth." After hearing these guys talk, I felt that Stan almost owed me an apology for giving me a hard time about yelling, "It's alive" yesterday. These guys were brutal. I sat with Roddy during break. He was loving the auxiliary route. He asked me how the flowers went over. I told him it was a good move and things appeared to be going well. Break time went by way too fast. I was back at route 19 and I stacked up two trays of bulk mail under the ledge as instructed by Stan. He called for a final sweep and I got everything racked. Lucy came by, and as I signed for my keys, I asked her how school was going. She was taking macroeconomics and found it a very hard class for the short summer session. Yesterday was the conclusion of week two and she had three more weeks to go. I congratulated her again on her accomplishment.

I pulled down my route and got my parcels—only one large parcel and two small ones. I went to route 44, and Chris Wojohowski told me he would have my piece ready in twenty minutes. He said the piece was really easy. I realize that it would be close to the Four Seasons Showroom, so now I had a reason to stop and see Janet and Chrissy. I took my mail out to the loading dock and backed up my jeep. I loaded route 19 into the jeep and went in to get my piece. I walked past the parcel section and wondered where Suzy Forecast was, curious to know her weather prediction.

I got my piece and headed out to my jeep. There were three carriers waiting to load their routes and were complaining about my jeep being there five minutes without moving. I apologized and loaded, then quickly moved the jeep. As I headed in to wash up and punch out, Steve Mueller complained, "That is two times this week that you dock-blocked me. It's disrespectful to leave your jeep at the dock."

"Sorry, bud, it won't happen again," was all I could offer.

"I would not do it again if I were you, Capeesh?" Steve warned. I left the office and headed to the piece, Smith Street. I liked business routes. They got a lot more mail, but the delivery was easy and most of the businesses were happy to see you. I finished in 45 minutes.

I headed over to the Four Seasons Showroom; but on the way, I stopped at Starbucks and picked up two frappuccinos. Janet mentioned the night before during our phone call that she and Chrissy loved them. I pulled up to Four Seasons and saw Janet. God, she looked great. She shrieked when she saw me. Perhaps I was taking too much credit, maybe she was more excited about Starbucks. Chrissy was on the phone and Janet waited for her to get off the phone to tell her, "Look, Chrissy, my boyfriend bought me two frappuccinos!"

I mumbled, "Well, one is for Chrissy." I was stunned, BOYFRIEND? I talked to her on the phone once and I was her boyfriend? One week on the job and I had a new best friend and a girlfriend I barely knew. Oh well, I figured I'd just go with the flow.

Chrissy was all smiles, "Good job, Kevin. You got major points. Major!"

Mr. Ford came out of his office and asked me, "Why can't you be our mailman? You are always here before our guy."

Janet complimented me on my t-shirt and asked what I was doing that night. I told her I was working until 5:00 p.m. She mentioned that her co-workers were going to happy hour at the bar around the corner right after work. I assured her that if I could make it I would surely be there. I said goodbye and Janet informed Chrissy that she was going to walk me to my jeep. She came around the counter, and man was this girl sexy! She was wearing a black dress that clung to her tight body and she was wearing a pair of very high heel, "fuck me" pumps. She's wearing quite a bit of make-up but not a lot. At least it was applied conservatively, just enough to make her look almost slutty. Janet grabbed my hand as we exited the building. She pointed out that you could see the bar from where we were standing. At the corner intersection on the cross street was a commercial bar, Bermuda Tradewinds. As we arrived at the jeep, she whispered in my ear, "I really want to see you there, I have a surprise for you," and then she kissed me on the cheek. She laughed and pointed to her cheek. "Lipstick," was all she said. I wiped my cheek and realized that I was getting aroused at this point.

Hurriedly, I got back in the jeep as I was developing a chubby. It didn't help as I watched her walk back to her job and marveled at how sexy she was. I was determined to have my way with her. Janet turned around when she got to the door and blew me a kiss. I turned my head as if I caught the kiss. We both laughed and waved goodbye.

At that point, I was at full mast and considered going to a restroom to do a selfie. I decided to drive to my route instead and hoped that I'd calmed down by then. I wondered what surprise she had in store for me. Now, I've seen Jerry Springer before so it dawned on me that my surprise could be that she was a man. There are transvestites that were as sexy as Janet. I was most certainly going to look for an Adam's apple the next time I saw her. Well, my chubby was completely gone by that point. I got to the route and started delivering mail. It was my third day on this route and I knew all the shortcuts. I was aware of the location of the mailboxes for the houses and if the house had a door slot. I was going up two steps at a time and hopping down steps. I had a real spring in my step and was really looking forward to happy hour.

I got to Fir Drive and Emma Lagone was waiting at her door. "Hello, Kenny. Do you want something to drink? It sure is hot."

I then realized that I was really thirsty. "Hello, Emma. Yes, it is hot. I'll tell you what, I'll finish this loop and come back. Oh, by the way, my name is Kevin."

Emma looked happy, "Yes, yes, come by. I'll get ready." Away I went to finish the loop and I realized that I was making great time and was way ahead of schedule. I made up about 45 minutes on the two-hour piece. Even after stopping to see Janet. It was only 12:30 and I only had an hour and a half of walking left. I didn't have to punch out until 5:00 p.m. So it was good that I was going to stop at Emma's. I finished the loop and I headed over there. I knocked at the door and Emma invited me in. I could swear she put on lipstick. Her house was nicely decorated and very neat. She had cheese and crackers out and asked me what I wanted to drink. I said I'll take a bottle of water and she offered, "Do you want a beer?"

I thought about it for a quick second and agreed, "A beer it is." Emma returned with a cold Budweiser and a glass. I mentioned that a glass was not necessary and took a swig straight from the bottle. Man, was that beer cold and satisfying.

Emma asked, "Should I turn the air-conditioning up? Walt used to like it cold in here."

"Yes, please," I responded as I munched on cheese and crackers and enjoyed another swig of beer. The air-conditioning felt good, and I was getting very comfortable. Emma was babbling about her grandkids in Arizona as I finished my beer.

She said, "Let me get you another."

I did not argue and made small talk while she was in the kitchen. "Arizona is very hot this time of year. I don't want to hear that it's a dry heat. One hundred ten degrees is still one hundred ten."

Emma commented, "I really miss my grandkids. I should move down there."

So I asked her, "Why don't you? What's keeping you here, the high taxes?" I grabbed the beer and scooped some more crackers. "Let's face it, during the day you're inside or you jump in the car and go to the store, A/C all the way. Man, I tell you, the letter carriers in Arizona have it rough. I personally would not want to do it." I looked over at Emma and could tell she wasn't interested in what I was saying. As comfortable as I was, I wanted to get back to the route. The longer you sat, the harder it was to get going again.

I chugged the second beer and told Emma that I had to finish the route. "Oh, Kenny, I wish you could stay. Walt would always come back when he finished the route."

"We'll see, Emma, but I need to thank you for the raincoat and galoshes yesterday. They really helped. My day would have been a lot worse if not for you. You really made my day."

Emma asked me, "Do you need a raincoat and galoshes? My dear departed Carmine has one someplace. I bet it would fit you."

I reminded her, "No, no, you actually gave me his raincoat yesterday. They fit perfectly. Don't you remember?"

She said, "I did? My goodness, I don't remember."

I thought, *The poor thing. She's starting to lose it.* I promised that if I had time I would come back. I said goodbye and headed out to the next loop. I was feeling good and decided that I was definitely going to happy hour tonight to see Janet. I was making really good time, and before I knew it, all I had left was the Fieldstone apartments and to empty the mailbox and then I was finito. I pulled up to the apartments. The way the loop was set up for the eighty apartments, you pulled around the back and parked by the opening in the middle. First loop was thirty-nine down. There were no steps to navigate and every apartment had the same large top-lifting mailbox that held a good deal of mail. Five feet away was the next box. Just raise the lid, deposit the

THANK GOD IT'S...NO BIG DEAL. IT'S FRIDAY | 135

mail, and on to the next. All the apartments had a door and a screen door. In some of the apartments, the inner door was open and if there was light in the apartment, you could see inside. Without light, it was hard to see inside unless you were really close. In some of the apartments with the door open you could smell the occupants cooking. I finished the down side and walked back to the jeep to get forty up. I was walking by the pool and wished I could jump in. I got back to the jeep and got the mail for the upside. Again, I was making good time; and at number 69, the door swung open.

I was startled. Oh shoot, it was the red menace, Sarah Jones. "When am I going to get a real melman? I'm going to call the Post Office and complain. Do you have it? Do you?" I forgot what she was talking about until she reminded me. "My letter from Justin Bieber. Do you know that I am the northeast chapter president of the Justin Bieber fan club? I am the number one Bieleber!"

I just mumbled, "Well, this is the mail that I have for you today," as I handed her the day's mail.

Jones exploded, "That letter is too important to give to a fake melman. You know that we saw your jeep on Fir Drive sitting there for 45 minutes. You're in big trouble, Mr. Fake Melman."

I lied when I said, "Well, Mrs. Lagone gave me some lemonade and cheese and crackers. You know, I do get a lunch break." While I was thinking, *It's none of this wacko's business.* I just said, "I've got to finish...I gotta go. Have a nice day."

I turned and walked away and heard her say, "I hate him."

I finished really fast and walked back to the jeep, all the while keeping an eye out for the red menace. I made it back to the jeep without incident. I drove over to the mailbox on Lafayette and emptied it. I had an hour and a half to kill before I had to punch out.

I was hungry and decided to go to the pizza place that Mick and I went to. I ordered two slices of pepperoni and a beer. I decided that I was going straight to the happy hour at Bermuda Tradewinds after work to hang out with Janet and her co-workers. I was eating the pizza when, out of the corner of my eye, I saw Steve Mueller. He was sitting in a booth, but I hadn't see him when I came in.

He said "Hey, you need to try the calamari here. It's so good."

All I could think to say was, "Will do" as Steve left. I didn't have time to tell him that I was not a seafood guy. Then I saw Maybel slide out of the same booth that Steve was in, and I was pretty sure they were sitting on the same side of that booth. Maybel smiled and waved.

I responded, "Hey Maybel," as she left with Steve. I was thinking, *That was weird*. Until it dawned on me that maybe, just maybe, they were involved. I didn't really care. It was none of my business. Who knows, maybe one or both of them was married. Once again, I didn't know or care. But, let me tell you, between Lamore, and Eugene and his wife having afternoon sex, it certainly appeared that letter carriers got laid more than the average profession. I finished eating, cleaned off the table, and thanked the pizza guy.

He introduced himself as Antonio and asked me in a heavy Italian accent, "Whata you, a newah mailaman? I never seena you before."

"I started on Monday and just finished my first week."

"Congratulations. I tella you what, nexta time, I buya you lunch."

I replied, "Thanks, Antonio. I'm gonna take you up on that. See you." As I drove back to the Post Office, I glanced at the gas tank. Wow, over half a tank. Ditt really screwed me with the parcels and not putting gas in the jeep.

I saw Mr. Portsmith as he jaywalked across the street. I recalled how he called me a jackass and was tempted to yell at him, but I thought better of it. I pulled up to the Post Office parking lot and parked the jeep. I put the outgoing mail in the bin on the dock and headed inside. The first person I saw was

Mike the Mortician. I really had to stop with the nickname. Mike smiled and asked, "How's it going?"

I told him that I was thrilled that the first week was over. He told me that he assigned me a locker, number 23. He gave me the locker combination and reached under the desk. Mike pulled out a brand new carrier mailbag. He handed it to me and advised, "Make sure you put your name on it or mark it with an identification. Some guys have tendencies to borrow things without asking or giving them back."

"I really appreciate this, Mike" as I slung the bag over my shoulder. I went to my route and put back the misracks, then headed to the bathroom/locker room. I saw my man Roddy there. He told me he did his auxiliary route and had to do four hours on Joey Rags' route. Joey had Union business. I proceeded to tell Roddy about my plans for the evening.

"You sly dog, You're moving fast. I would come as your wingman, but I have things to do. Did you get a locker?" I told him that I did. I was thinking that I could use a wingman.

Roddy said, "Check us out. We are really moving up in the world." The locker room was occupied by a couple of carriers who overheard our conversation.

Theo laughed, "Hear that, Syd? The new guys are moving up in the world."

Syd responded, pointing up, "Yeah, moving up in this dump."

Roddy shrugged it off and said, "Hey, guys, Thank God it's Friday, although we work tomorrow."

Theo looked at me and said, "Hey, you made quite an impression on Silverstein when you did my piece the other day. Don't pay her any attention; but do not, I repeat, do not walk across her or her mother's lawn."

"I'll try to remember."

Roddy asked me, "Are you going straight to happy hour?"

I replied that if I went home I'd be losing valuable happy

hour time and, at best, getting there at 6:30. "I've got another new t-shirt that's clean and dry."

Syd pointed at his locker and offered, "Hey, I have a shirt here that would fit you. You are welcome to borrow it." Syd pulled out a solid black dress shirt that looked and fit perfectly when I tried it on. I wondered if I was going to point wherever I went if I wore his shirt.

The guys were all giving me advice when Lamore walked in. He asked, "Do you have a date?"

"I'm meeting some people on the route for happy hour." Lamore opened his locker, reached in, and came out with a top of the line cologne.

"Only use a little. It's really strong. People will be able to smell you coming for two blocks."

Theo exclaimed, "That's how his conquests know he is on his way." Everybody laughed.

I spritzed myself a couple of times. "Thanks, bro," as I handed the cologne back to him.

Lamore teased, "Don't do anything I wouldn't do."

Theo chimed in, "DO whatever Bobby would do," as everybody in the locker room laughed.

We all went our separate ways as we exited the locker room.

I went to the window to finish clearing and turn in my keys. It was almost 5:00 p.m., and I headed to the punch clock. There were about 12 guys mulling around, ready to go home. I heard somebody say, "Check it out. The new guy is all dolled up." A guy puts on a shirt and that becomes the focal point of conversation.

Roddy explained my intentions, "He has a date. This guy moves fast. He could be the second coming of Lamore."

Lamore asked, "What do you mean by that?" Everybody laughed.

"We all get ours," said Del Greco.

Quentin responded, "Sure, mona, sure."

The clock hit 5:00 p.m. and we started punching out. A

couple of the guys wished me luck as they headed to their cars to go home. Roddy and I were the last to punch out, and we walked to the parking lot together.

Roddy asked, "Do you have condoms?"

"No, but I barely know this girl."

He explained, "Yes, but when alcohol is involved, inhibitions drop. I heard when a female drinks she relaxes, and they get wet down there. It is so much easier to get laid."

I mentioned, "Lord knows that I am overdue! I certainly hope that I do. Maybe I'll pick some up on the way. You should have brought up the condom thing earlier. Lamore must have a case of them."

"I wonder how many condoms he uses in a week?" Neither one of us said anything as I was sure we were both trying to calculate that number.

We got to our cars and I said, "I'll see you tomorrow. And you will get all the details, full disclosure, my friend."

I stopped at a convenience store to get my package of raincoats, you know, condoms. The bar was only 20 minutes away, but there was massive traffic. It was in the business section of town and most of the employees were leaving work and going home. I sat at a traffic light for eight minutes due to congestion. I finally got to Bermuda Tradewinds, and the parking lot was full. I parked all the way in the back as if I got the very last spot.

As I walked to the bar, I felt a little apprehensive. I definitely could have used a wingman. I entered the bar and the music and alcohol-fueled conversation was loud. There were people at tables and the bar was stacked. There were 30 or 40 people in the corner and I saw Mr. Ford, so I headed in that direction. I did not see Janet, but Ford noticed me and waved me over. He looked buzzed. His suit jacket was off and his shirt and tie were open. "Hey, it's Flavor." As I mentioned, it was loud and I thought to myself, *Did he say flavor?*

I extended my hand to him. "Hey Ford, how are you doing? By the way, my name is Kevin."

After all, he was not my boss and we are not at his business so I wasn't going to call him Mr. Ford.

He just said, "Huh, sure, let's do shots and I'll buy you a drink." Although I had three beers over the course of the day, I was a little tight. Hey, I didn't know these people. Ford turned to me, "I'm doing vodka. That good for you? Get whatever you want."

I agreed, "Hell, yeah, vodka."

Ford said, "Call me Ernie. You want a beer or a drink? Get Flavor whatever he wants on me." There he goes with that flavor stuff again; but Ernie, his name is Ernie Ford?

I went with the flow, "You got it, Erndog, I'll take a Bud." What the heck, the man was buying. We did our shots and clanked our beers. Ernie was babbling on about the Post Office and his opinions on its employees. I saw Chrissy standing with her back to me standing at the corner of the bar. This girl had an awesome silhouette.

My boy Ernie Ford, who was feeling no pain, yelled, "Warren, come over here and have a shot with me and Flavor of the Month." I heard him clearly now and realized he was talking about Janet and me. He turned to me, "Come on, Flavor, let's do another shot."

"What did you call me?"

Warren came over and ordered a scotch and talked to Ford while the shots were being poured. I interrupted them, "What did you call me?"

He made the statement, "Oh, you don't know," as he put the shot glasses in front of us. Ford yelled, "Bonzai" as he and Warren gulped their shots. I was still waiting for a response when they both started shouting, "Shot, shot, shot!" So I downed my shot and as soon as I was done, I felt my face getting pulled to the side. It was Janet and she planted a kiss on my lips.

She said, "Hey, babe, I am so glad you came. I love your shirt." She was so sexy and I noticed she was a little buzzed.

Suddenly, I recalled what Roddy said about women and

alcohol. I was feeling the shots already and said to her, "I'm really glad I'm here, too."

She grabbed my hand and said," Let's say hello to Chrissy." She pulled me towards the corner of the bar.

I heard Ford say, "So long, Flavor, you lucky son of a bitch." He seemed way too concerned about Janet and me.

We got to the corner of the bar where the Four Seasons crew had gathered. It was mostly guys, and they stood out with their Four Seasons polo or t-shirts. The back of the t-shirt read, "Ask me the reasons you should choose Four Seasons."

Chrissy came over and gave me a hug, "Thanks for that frappuccino the other day. I'm in training and had to make that day my cheat day. I can hardly wait for tomorrow night." I told her that I was not at all familiar with their music. She asked me who I listened to. I informed her Metallica, Rancid, and Alice in Chains. She told me, "You are going to enjoy them then. Only harder and faster."

"Sounds good," I replied.

Janet came over and asked me, "How was your day?" I started telling her about the red menace and she seemed distant, perhaps more interested in something or somebody in the Four Seasons crowd. She excused herself and Chrissy came over. She said she was leaving as she had to get up early and go for a run and then go to the gym. She then planned to take a nap before the show. I told her that sounded like a full day and I bid her adieu. I finished my beer and ordered another. I saw Chrissy talking to Janet and some guy from Four Seasons.

The guy was big, maybe a little smaller than Quentin. I heard Ford. He was ten feet away and wasted. I recalled the "Flavor" comment. I guess he was implying that Janet dated a lot and I was the current guy. My insecurities set in, and I assumed she must have recently broken up with someone from work and I was invited here to make the guy jealous or, at least, to use me as leverage. It made me wonder where I was in this aspiring relationship.

I felt like an outsider and considered leaving. I saw Chrissy walking out of the bar. Janet came over and forced me against the wall and started to kiss me. I normally don't make out in public, but I was horny and went along with it. Again, I wondered if this display of affection was intended to piss off a co-worker ex of hers. I let her grind for a while. After a minute or two I came up for air. I turned her around and now she was against the wall. I took a swig of beer and asked her, "So who here is your ex? You can point him out, I just want to see what your type is. I'm not the jealous type."

She looked at me and sternly replied, "So you want to talk? I was in the mood for something else. If this is your desire, let's go out to your car. This could be fun." She grabbed my hand, and we headed for the door. We walked past the Four Seasons crew toward the end of the bar. She was moving quickly as we headed out the door. She turned to me and asked, "So you want to know who I dated at Four Seasons? Chrissy, I dated Chrissy." She was laughing as I wondered, *How I can talk her into a threesome.*

"Would you like that if I dated Chrissy? Where is your car? No, I did not date Chrissy. I'm strictly dickly."

Damn! was my gut reaction. I just said, "My car is over there by the Bermuda Tradewinds sign." We reached my car and I opened the door for her. I went around to the driver's side and got in. I was beyond buzzed by now. Janet was a little pissed off and she looked really hot.

I kind of leaned in for a kiss or at least a peck. She put a finger on my lips. "Hell no, you want to talk? That's what you want? You're not the jealous type? Good! I have dated a couple of guys from Four Seasons. But let me tell you something, when I do get involved with someone, I am monogamous. I expect the same. I do not fool around. Because when the relationship is over, it's over. If we do get together and you want to be with someone else, fine, we part ways. Absolutely no hard feelings. But you never call me again, we are over. No more, never again. I am not going to cling to something that is not working. I've had guys beg me to take them back. They're usually drunk and want another fling. Nope! One chance and I am done, my friend. I'm a very desirable girl and will find someone else and move on. Now, how about you?"

My head was spinning. My God, this girl was so desirable and, oh boy, did I desire her. Now I've never been a cheater. Well, there was this time with an older woman who pretty much wouldn't take no for an answer. And a little flirting here and there, but I was not going to tell Janet that. Of course, I was going to tell her whatever she wanted to hear right now. I said, "I am not a cheater. I want trust and to be able to trust whomever I am involved with. I have to admit what bothers me most is that Ford kept calling me Flavor of the Month. I mean, what's up with that?"

"You really want to know?" she asked. "Do you think you can handle it?"

"Look, I really like you, so you might as well tell me."

So she told me her story. "I've been working at Four Seasons for a year and a half. I have an associate degree from SUNY. My cousin is a realtor in Bethpage and she is making a fortune. She inspired me to get my realtor's license. I figured, why rack up more student loans? So I work at Four Seasons and am taking the realtor class. Mr. Ford, well Ernie, wasn't married at the time and we dated. He cheated and he ended up marrying the girl he cheated on me with. Let me tell you, he does want to fool around again. It's over, I guess that's where his animosity lies. He even offered to be my sugar daddy. Can you believe that? I went out with a guy from marketing. We went out a couple of times, but I'm almost positive Ford got him to end it. Then there is a really nice guy in the warehouse. Big Lou. you might have seen me talking to him at the bar. He wants to go out. Now, I bet the sex would be amazing; but he is so, and I hate to admit that I am so shallow and God forgive me, but he is so dumb. I can't get past that. I cannot have a halfway decent conversation with him. His only interests are the Yankees and NASCAR. I can't, I can't. I really enjoyed our conversation the other night. You are funny and witty, and you appear to be smart."

This beautiful girl was sexy and extremely insightful. I said, "So you and Ford, well, Ernie. I can't believe his name is Ernie Ford. Like Tennessee Ernie Ford."

She said, "I know, I know." We both laughed and she looked so beautiful that I leaned in to kiss her and she kissed me back. She pulled away, "Your turn. Let's hear about you."

"Okay, okay, well I have not dated anybody, and I repeat anybody, from Four Seasons. Although I am interested in this hot, sexy, future real estate agent there. My last relationship was with a girl in Texas while I was stationed there. She was three years older than me. She wanted me to re-enlist. I was ready to get out of the Army and did not want to re-enlist. We both knew that a long-distance relationship would not work out, so here I am."

Janet seemed to be hanging on every word I said. She smiled, her eyes sparkling, and she asked me, "Are you ready for your surprise? Are we going to do this?"

As I started to say, "I'm in," we grabbed each other. She reached over and reclined the driver's seat. She got on top and straddled me as we made out. Just as I was trying to figure out how to get her panties off and a condom on, Janet explained, "I'm having my period. It's the last day." I was definitely disappointed.

As I was about to lie and say that it was okay, she rolled off me and said, "Pull down your pants." I did not say a word as I obliged her. I reclined my seat even more and little Kevin sprang into action. Janet hovered over me and said, "Good, nice and clean." She then proceeded to give me the best head I'd ever gotten. I mean, good God, this little angel was licking, slurping, and moaning. It was obvious this was not the first time she'd done this. No wonder Ford was sad. He would never experience this again. I was in heaven. It didn't take long, so I figured that I should warn her. "I'm coming." I said louder, "I'm coming." I couldn't take it anymore and screamed, "I'm coming!" as I exploded into her mouth.

She continued to go about her business, slurping until I could take no more. I was shaking as she raised up, opened the door, and spit out. I was spent. I think I saw stars.

Janet closed the door and leaned over to me. "Kiss me." I immediately pulled away from her, repulsed. She laughed and said, "Just kidding. Let's just say some guys like it. I didn't think you would."

I was still reeling. I swear that I will never cheat. I had a girlfriend in the past who asked me, "Why do guys cheat? If the girlfriend was always willing, why do men have to stray? Isn't sex basically the same?" I imagine on the bell curve of sex, most of the time it is. But this blow job was at the beginning of the curve. Well, some guys needed the variety or the conquest. I knew that I would always want access to this girl's talent. I grabbed Janet and hugged, just held her. I mumbled, "Wow."

She hugged me back and asked, "Do you have gum or a mint?"

"If you look in the glove compartment, there's gum" I commented. Whatever she wanted, she got. She took a piece of Trident gum and asked, "Do you want to go back inside?"

"I'll probably be leaving soon." I responded, "I'm not sure I can walk. Would it be okay if I went home? I have to work tomorrow and Sunday, too, plus I'm a little tired. But I'm so glad I came here tonight."

Janet was looking in the mirror, "Are you good to drive?"

"Oh, yeah, you just sobered me up. Let me walk you to the door."

"No, no, you don't have to."

I got out of the car and grabbed her hand, "I don't have to, I want to." As we walked hand in hand back to the entrance, we made plans for Saturday night. A quick peck on the lips and we departed. When I got back to my car, there was a commotion at the bar entrance. A large man was manhandling Ford as a cab pulled up. Ford was not going quietly. He was screaming some nonsense. I don't know if the other guy was Big Lou or a bouncer. The big guy forcefully got Ford into the back seat of the cab and closed the door. I heard Ford yell, "I just want to speak with Janet!" as the cab drove away. He was really missing what I just got. It made me think, *I don't know what I am getting myself into, but I'm going to enjoy the ride.*

I wanted to test myself before I drove. My cousin Peter was a Nassau County cop, and he told me to raise one foot off the ground and see if I could balance myself. He said if you can't do that, do not drive. I was solid so I got in the car and drove home one happy Mother... It was only 7:30 and I didn't have a long drive. I was home before 8:00.

Mom made chicken and rice and I ate it with a soda. I took a shower and brushed my teeth. I almost did a selfie in the shower but decided to save it for tomorrow night. I gave Janet a call before I went to bed. She told me that she was thinking of me. I said, "Ditto, well not ditto because that would mean that I was thinking of me, too. No, baby, I cannot get you off my mind, and I don't want to." We both laughed and she mentioned that Ford was wasted when she went back to the bar. They had to escort him out. We chatted about more important things for a half-hour and then said goodnight to each other.

OH, IT'S SATURDAY, IT'S SATURDAY

Next thing I knew, the alarm startled me when it went off at 5:20. I hit the snooze and thought of Janet. I was raging hard so I took a shower to wake up and rubbed one out. Today officially started week number two of my postal career. Last Monday seemed like ages ago. I excitedly got dressed, partly because I was going to see Morbid Obesity, but mostly because I would see my baby again. I wondered if the sex could be that great again. Only one way to find out, and I intended to find out. I was driving to the Post Office and had extra time so I stopped at the McDonald's. I ordered a fast-food breakfast sandwich and was eating it as I drove in the parking lot.

I saw Catfish Tommy Moore. It was only 6:15 as I casually went in. There were eight guys and two gals waiting to punch in. First, there was the Morbid Obesity crew, Pittman, Yates, and Joey Ramonski. Maybel and Dotty were off to one side; and Del Greco, Steve Graves, Benjy, and Quentin were right up front. Del Greco asked Benjy, "Have you seen Trixie?"

Benjy replied, "No, not in a while."

Steve Graves asked, "Isn't she that hooker?"

Maybel seemed annoyed as she commented, "The proper term is sex worker. Let's show her a little dignity."

"Oh, yeah, sex worker. Let's face it, she's a crackhead who has sex for money," Quentin retorted.

Benjy replied, "Regardless of what we call her, she's a mess. Who knows what diseases she has. Speaking of diseases, I have a mole on my leg. I bet it's melanoma."

Steve Graves chimed in, "When did we stop calling a spade a spade? Pretty soon, a murderer will be a population control specialist."

Del Greco added, "Or a rapist will be called an uninvited vaginal guest. I personally am sticking with hooker."

There were still eight minutes to go and Wojohowski came in. Quentin loudly asked, "Where's your house key?"

Wojo then asked, "Hey, Q, are we talking about hookers?"

Joey Ramonski called out, "Hey, Chris, what time is soundcheck?"

Wojo responded, "5:15 like always."

Eugene and Roddy walked in. It was two minutes to punch in.

Joey Ramonski addressed the group, "Hey now. At the Modern bar tonight at 9:00, Morbid Obesity. I hope to see everybody there. We are having music executives there. So let's all show up and support the guys."

Quentin Roosevelt said, "Oh, yeah, I'm looking forward to it. I'm going to take attendance and personally be offended if you don't show," to nobody in particular.

It was one minute before punching in. Quentin punched in and said, "I like to be first. It's easier to follow me." A couple of guys were walking through the swinging door just as the clock struck 6:30. MacGregor, Joey Rags, and Syd just made it and got in line to punch in.

I glanced at the carrier supervisor's desk and noticed that Mike was there. I found out later that Stan rarely worked on Saturday. When it was my turn to punch in, it was actually 6:32; but my card displayed 6:33. Again, the Post Office used one hundred units and not sixty minutes. They gave us eight units to account for clock congestion. As I punched in, there were still carriers coming into the office. I went to route 19 and started racking letters. After two trays, or four feet of mail, I needed to go to the restroom. I went, did my business, and washed my already dirty hands. As I was walking back to the route, I was right in front of the punch clock. Mike was talking to George the Bird and MacGregor was heading towards the break room with a coffee cup in his hand. The swinging doors opened and Mick walked through. He was walking fast like always.

MaGgregor noticed him and let loose, "Good afternoon, Irish. You are late, I guess there's no app for that, you know, being on time for work. Perhaps we fell off the wagon."

Mick punched in and said, "Car wouldn't start."

MacGregor replied, "Yeah, right."

Mike quipped, "Glad you could make it, Mick."

I went back to my route, well, my route until Friday. The open bidding for the route ended yesterday, and management would announce who won the bid on Monday. Next Saturday, the new "melman" will start route 19 and I would be someplace else. I was getting very proficient at racking route 19. I immediately knew if a letter was a misracked. I knew all the correct names on East Chestnut.

I was racking the mail at a really good clip. Then I heard my first P. Ennis family of the day. I wondered if Ms. Cummings was working today. The atmosphere was so much lighter today. There was still lots of energy but definitely looser. Maybe the absence of Stan was why. Mike came by and told me to clean up the route and take the bulk mail I left yesterday. He gave me the key to the door for when I worked tomorrow. I signed for it and he gave me a list of the mailboxes that I had to empty tomorrow.

He explained, "As far as express mail goes, deliver the business if they are open. If it's residential, make an attempt. Bring everything back here to the window and leave non-deliverable express mail and delivered slips. You'll be fine. We don't usually get a lot of express, but you never know. You should be done in two hours."

I told him, "I'm so glad you reminded me, Mike. It's been an awfully long week."

He asked me, "You are scheduled to be off on Tuesday. Do you want to come in for overtime? It's summertime, after all, and we have six carriers on vacation. For the rest of the summer, we are going to have eight carriers out every week until September. Be prepared to work lots of overtime."

I thought, *Overtime, time and a half, cha-ching!* I needed the cash. I didn't have anything better to do than make money, so I sucked up to Mike, "Anything that I can do for you, Mike. Whatever you need, bro. I'll be there Tuesday."

"Thanks, Kevin," he said as he walked away. It was almost 8:00 a.m. and I heard a horn honk. "Break!" Like lemmings, the carriers headed to the coffee truck. From behind me, I heard Mick explaining how his car battery died and he had to call triple A. "They came and I had to buy a new battery. Set me back a hundred and fifty bucks. It figures, I just finished the payments on the car and the battery dies, figures."

Roddy came out of the business aisle, and I said, "Yo, bro, how's it hanging?"

Del Greco was right behind me and responded, "Hanging to the left, thanks for asking."

Roddy said, "There's Eric."

Yo-yo was gimping through the swinging door towards us. He stopped when he saw us, "Yo, muchachos, como estás?"

Roddy responded, "Muy bien."

Eric was like, "Let's hit the roach coach."

I reminded him, "Shouldn't you punch in first?"

"Yo, Kev, you are right, as usual. I'll see you at the truck, yo." He turned and gimped through the swinging doors with a purpose.

Roddy and I walked towards the coffee truck and he asked, "So how did it go last night?"

"So much better than expected. You need to be sitting down when I tell you."

Yo-yo appeared to be moving with some difficulty, but he was covering lots of ground pretty well.

He asked, "Yo, who's paying, yo?"

I said, "It's your turn."

"Whoa, Kev, you know I'm busted. Yo, pregnant wife and all that, yo."

I said, "Yeah, yeah, yeah, nobody's got it harder than you sitting in the air-conditioning all day. I'm buying. I had an awesome time last evening. Epic!"

We got to the coffee truck, and the coffee truck guy and the carriers were carrying on verbally like the clerks, only more cerebral than the savages inside. I was already getting into the carrier versus clerk mentality.

The coffee truck guy saw us and said, "Hey, it's the new guys! You're still here. You made it through the first week, congrats." I grabbed a blueberry muffin and a diet coke. Roddy got a fruit cup, and Yo-yo was taking his time grabbing things, then putting them back.

Coffee truck guy said, "I'm going out on a limb here. Let me guess, the mooch here is paying."

I told him, "No, I got this."

Eric said, "I'm done" and showed the coffee truck guy a soda, a juice, egg sandwich, and a bag of chips.

The coffee truck guy said, "Just give me fifteen dollars. I gave you the mooch discount. Take it easy, guys. Have a great weekend. I'll see you Monday, if you make it."

I responded, "Thanks, bro. You, too."

We headed into the office and, as always, the cool air felt good. We sat down at Roddy's auxiliary route located in the business section. He said, "Okay, I am so ready to hear about last night's escapades. Remember, Kev, full disclosure. I want to know everything. Every little detail."

"Brace yourself, my brother, brace yourself."

Eric chimed in, "Guys, I went to the doctor yesterday. He told me that this issue with my hip could be permanent. He might have to operate."

All I could say was, "Well, what's the diagnosis?"

"Well, it pops out of the socket. I feel it click."

Roddy stated, "All of this because you slipped on bird shit? You do know that people think you might be faking it. I want to hear about Kevin's date last night."

Eric said, "Well, I have to listen to the doctors, I don't care what people think."

Roddy added, "We are not here to judge you, Eric. I just hope you feel better. You do know that doctors need work to make their money. You need to get a second or third opinion."

"Yo, word up," Eric responded, "a guy has a doctor's appointment and you miss out on so much around here. Yo, Kev, you had a date, yo?"

"You sound surprised, Eric. Plus, you are really using 'yo' a lot."

Eric rationalized, "Yeah, but I'm not answering phones right now, yo."

"It's about practice, Eric. You sound surprised that I went out. I guess you could call it a date." So I filled in Yo-yo how I met Janet and her co-workers from Four Seasons during happy hour at Bermuda Tradewinds. I mentioned how Ford was the owner's son and Janet's boss and that he was buying me drinks and it was loud and he called me Flavor.

Eric says "Yo, Kev is Flavor Flav."

I responded, "No, I wasn't sure what he said at first. Then I pieced together that she might be the office slut. I was also wondering if I was invited to make one or more of her exes jealous. I was a little angry but also very buzzed."

Roddy put in his two cents, "Be very careful, my friend."

I told him, "I'm a big boy and far from stupid. I asked her who she used to date and that I had some questions as to why I was even there. So we go out to my car to talk. She explained how when she first started working there, Ford asked her out. So they did get involved, but he cheated. They broke up and he married the girl he cheated on her with. Then she went out with two of the guys who work there. Ford kind of put the kibosh on her dating them. I did see one of the warehouse workers she dated, no sex, she said."

Roddy said, "She says no sex but we don't know that for sure. Oh, boy."

Yo-yo urged, "Go on, go on. Yo, with wifey very pregnant, I haven't gotten any in months. I'm living vicariously through you, Kev."

I told them that I was slightly drunk and Janet looked so hot and I was beyond horny. So I figured, she is who she is, and I'm not signing any contracts. So we started kissing. She informed me that It was "that time of the month." She then proceeded to give me the best blowjob of my life, by far. I explained how she let me come in her mouth.

I didn't know that DelGreco was walking behind me and had heard the last statement. He stopped and asked, "Do you guys know what the two most often told lies are? First, the check is in the mail. Second is, I won't come in your mouth."

At that instant, somebody yelled, "Break over!" So, before I headed back to route 19, Roddy asked me, "Are you going to see her again?"

I let him know, "Yes, tonight. We are going to see Morbid Obesity. We're going to meet up there. Her friend is a huge fan and Yates said I can get them introductions. Are you going?"

"No, I have a family function. My nephew is graduating from high school. Puerto Rican families, well at least mine, are very close. It's bad enough that I cannot attend the ceremony; but if I missed the party because I was going to a bar, it's unacceptable. My advice to you, my friend, is to be careful, be very careful.

Yo-yo said, "Yo, Kev, I'm so happy for you. You are my hero and my best friend." He was still on that best friend routine. He seemed very impulsive so I didn't think it would be long until I was replaced.

Mortician Mike walked by and said, "Eric, if you are able, can you help out on route 16?"

Yo-yo said, "I'll see you guys later, yo. And Kev, thanks for breakfast and lunch."

I headed back to route 19; and as soon as I got there, Mike called for a final flat sweep.

Again, I felt the mood in the office to be lighter. The guys were laughing and joking more, although still uber focused. I was feeling it, too, and noticed that I was walking a little slower. Stegman could be doing laps around me. As I went to sweep, I looked up and noticed the perimeter of the ceiling. I took notice of the one-way mirrors that Letterman and Joey Rags warned us about. I was curious to know if somebody was behind them and watching. I assumed not today. Even the clerks were subdued. Suzy Forecast wasn't even bringing up the weather. She was laughing and saying once again, "Goodness, we so need to write a book about this place. I doubt anybody would believe it." I got all my flats and it was about half full. Mike looked at my cart and made a notation on his clipboard. I got back to 19 and after 45 minutes I was done with my flats and started pulling them down.

Mike came over and asked me how I was doing and if I could do an hour on Mike Pittman's route. "Take as much bulk mail as you can. Take an hour on this route and do an hour on Pitt's route. Pittman wants to go home early. It's a huge night for the guys. I'm going to try to make it, myself. You should try to go."

"I have every intention of going. I've heard only good things about them."

"Thanks, Kevin. Hopefully, I will see you there." As he turned, he almost knocked over Lucy Consuelo Nieves-Gonzales Martinez Smith.

"Good morning, Mike. It's nice bumping into you," my favorite angel said.

"You, too, Lucy," he replied as they went their separate ways.

I pulled down my flats and put them in trays. I then proceeded over to Pittman to see about the piece that I was getting. As I got there, I saw Roddy and said, "Hey, bud, I'm getting an hour on Pittman's route."

Roddy responded, "Only one? I'm getting two."

Pittman looked up and asked, "Who is getting the deuce?"

Roddy said that it was him.

Pittman nodded, "Over there," as he pointed to three trays. "Yours is over there, J. I'm going to see you later, right?"

There was a little over one tray. I said, "Yeah, buddy. I'm looking forward to it."

Pittman admitted, "I have to say I'm a little nervous."

I said, "Um, Mike, my girlfriend's friend is big, big fan. I was wondering if you could kind of say hello to her. She would be thrilled."

He responded, "Yeah, that's what Yates was talking about right. Okay, bring her backstage, I'll say hello, but you might want to tell her that I have a serious girlfriend. But sure, I'll accommodate you."

"Thanks, Mike. I'm getting major points for this, major!" I carried the hour piece back to route 19 just as Lucy was bringing her cart down the aisle. I caught the end of DelGreco and her going at it; and it sounded like Lucy got the best of him, as usual. The guys in that aisle were laughing their asses off, and DelGreco said he was going to the bathroom. I'm imagining it was for a selfie. This guy was a real perv. It was one thing whacking off, but you don't have to announce it.

I threw my remaining letter-size until Lucy came by with the accountables. I signed for two certified and the mailbox key. I told Lucy that I missed seeing her when I came back to the office last night.

She answered, "That's so sweet. Have a good day." I melted as she walked away, and I debated Lucy or Janet, as if there was a choice. Well, Lucy made my heart race just by being in her presence. Janet, on the other hand, was sexy as hell and appeared to really like me. I doubt Lucy could perform like Janet, but I wouldn't mind giving it a go. *Wouldn't mind?*, I said to myself. I wa dying to know.

The rest of the morning went smoothly. I was able to take all of the bulk mail, and I'll end up being a little less than an hour late leaving the office. So, with the Pittman piece, I'm good for two hours overtime. I washed up and checked my parcels. There was one large parcel and four small ones. I saw Suzy Forecast and joked with her, "Suzy, you're killing me with the parcels."

She said, "Sorry, Kevin, But it is going to be a fabulous day. No rain and not too hot."

I kind of put my foot in my mouth when I asked, "Suzy, you seem really interested in the weather, do you spend a lot of time outdoors?"

Through all the make-up Suzy explained, "Not since I lost my husband." She proceeded to tell me her sad tale. Suzy was from Finland and loved to ski. She was so good that she was going to be in the Olympics. During trials, she crashed into a tree. She suffered total amnesia—completely lost her memory. She explained that it was tough; but after a couple of years, she was making great progress. It was then that her husband committed suicide. Suzy always felt that the burden of him having to help her contributed to his demise, and she still carried the grief and guilt.

All I could utter was, "I am so, so sorry for you."

She said, "It was then that I started working for the Post Office, and I am able to help out the carriers by alerting them to the weather." All I knew was that I would never hear her tell us about the weather the same, and I'll appreciate it more.

I loaded up my jeep and headed out. I was very conscious about space at the dock. I didn't want Steve Mueller getting bent out of shape. He did have a point. I guess that I would have a problem with it if I was waiting. I stopped at the 7-Eleven and bought some drinks. Note to self: "Self, get a cooler bag and buy drinks in bulk and save a ton of money."

I started delivering mail, and right away, I noticed the difference between working on Saturday and a weekday. On Saturday, residents were home. There were so many more of you, and you all had something to say. "You're early" or, more often, "you're late." There was no set time that you're supposed to get the mail. Here's one of your favorites, "You can keep the bills. All we want is the checks." Some people asked about Walt. I've spoken with the man two times. For the most part, you all knew more about him than me. Maybe you can tell me how he is. I didn't really like the guy after the way he left the route.

I went to drop off the big box on Spruce. Although it was large, it was very light. I pulled up in the jeep and the homeowner was in the garage. I noticed on the parcel that it was addressed to Phil Frith. He saw me and called out, "Alright, it made it for the barbeque. I wasn't sure it would make it. Thanks again, buddy. You have to stop by later, I'll cook you a burger." He took the box and opened it. I was ultra-curious to know what was in the box. He took out a tall chef's hat with the Yankees logo on it. He was beaming, "And they're playing Boston tonight. Somebody's going to be ready, uh-huh, this guy. I'm telling you, guy, you gotta stop by for a burger!" I assured him that I would.

I got back to the route and started delivering the mail again. I was thinking of Janet and her magic mouth as I delivered. It was not too hot today, but I was sweating a little more than usual. I delivered to Fir Drive and, luckily, Emma's door was closed. I really wanted to finish. When I got to the other side, Emma was at the door and she called out, "Kenny, Kenny!" I waved but kept walking. Now, I felt a little guilty about blowing her off, as I did say that I would stop by as much as possible. But it was Kevin who made the promise, and she's calling for Kenny. It was Kenny who didn't stop. Maybe I'll go back later. After all, I had a date with a burger and I still had that piece on Pittman's route. I just kept delivering the mail on the route. Before I knew it, I just had the apartments and the mailbox left on this route. I parked in the usual spot in the back middle of the apartments. I did the first loop and, for the first time, the pool was hopping. There were hot bodies in bikinis and bodies that had absolutely no business being in a two-piece. There was a group of muffin tops by the gate. Radios were playing and kids were playing and doing that pool scream. I finished that first loop fast and two people actually waved to me. I waved back as I headed to the jeep. On the second loop, the second apartment had a certified. I knocked, but no one answered and I left that yellow notice slip. I got to Sarah Jones' apartment. I was ready for anything, but there was no sign of the red menace. I wondered if she was at the pool. Man, I wanted to be in the pool. I finished the apartments in less than half an hour and headed back to the jeep.

It was not even 2:00 and as I emptied the mailbox, I debated, Pittman piece or Frith's first. I was really thirsty so I went to Frith's first. That was a pretty good tongue twister— Frith's first. Try to say that three times fast. So I headed to Frith's first. I parked in front of the residence and walked down the driveway to the garage. I could see inside the garage and was impressed with Friths' man cave/garage. There was quite a bit of Yankee memorabilia. I went to the wooden gate next to the garage and yelled, "Anybody home?"

Mrs. Frith came out and said, "We already got our mail. Is there anything else?"

Phil Frith met her at the gate and said, "Hey, buddy! You came, good. Babe, I invited him when he delivered my chef's hat." Frith was proudly wearing it.

"Oh, the hat," wifey Frith said as she rolled her eyes.

He offered, "Grab a beer or soda. There are chips, help yourself. I'll get you a burger. We're putting steaks on at four."

I responded "Thanks, bro. The hat looks good on you." I grabbed a Diet Coke and some chips. There were eight people sitting on Frith's picnic tables. I sat down and quickly became the topic of conversation.

"Why does a stamp cost so much?" someone inquired. Now, in the breakroom there was a poster that showed the prices of stamps worldwide. In most European countries, the price of a stamp was eighty cents to over a dollar. Japan cost eighty to ninety cents for a first-class letter. The poster also showed how all these smaller countries together fit inside an outline of the continental United States. I schooled them that a fifty-two cent stamp from here in New York to Hawaii, fuhgetaboutit. Letterman would be so proud of me right now. There was an attractive brunette named Donna in her late thirties who stated, "Now, I live on North Chestnut. When our regular guy is off, we get mail for East and West Chestnut. Why three Chestnuts in the same town is my question." I told her that it boggled my mind. "And if they had to have three Chestnuts, they could have used different numbers. Numbers are infinite, absolutely no reason to use the same numbers."

Frith came over, "Here's your burger. I put cheese on it, I hope that's okay."

"Of course, it is."

Frith shouted out, "Anybody else want a burger or a dog? There are some ready."

One guy said, "I'll take one of each, please, Phil. Well done, burn them."

I bit into the cheeseburger. It was juicy and delicious. I thought, *Phil? Phil Frith*. Okay. I was devouring this burger when Phil came over, "The fixings are over here. Dude, you are going to need another burger. Consider it on its way." As I got another soda, Phil brought me my second burger. "Here you go, buddy, I didn't catch your name." I told him Kevin and Phil asked me, "So Kev, are you going to be our regular carrier from now on?"

I explained that I only started at the Post Office on Monday and quickly touched on the bidding process. New people arrived and Donna yelled, "Tina!" Donna was wearing high heels and a pair of white shorts and I could see her thong through the shorts. Tina and Donna hugged almost too long. I was almost finished with my second burger and I wanted to get to that Pittman piece.

I thanked Phil and said goodbye to the group and left through the gate. I was almost at the jeep when Donna called out, "Excuse me, Kevin. If you are ever over on North Chestnut, why don't you stop by. Here's my number. Give me a call."

I ask her, "Wasn't that your husband sitting next to you?"

Donna replied, "Oh no, we're kind of separated. Staying together for the kids. He's cool with it, though. Oh, you didn't know. We're swingers. This is a mingle party. If you're not doing anything around 8:00 tonight, things are going to get happening."

Holy shit, this mailman gig was crazy and created lots of sexual opportunities. After all, we interacted with lots of people. The average route was three hundred houses; and apparently, some of these houses contained desperate housewives. Confucious said, "Luck is when opportunity meets preparation." So I guess sexy luck was when desire met opportunity. I told Donna that I was busy tonight but hoped to see her again really soon over on North Chestnut. She smiled and turned to head to the backyard. Suddenly, I thought of Janet and her threat that I would never get a hum job like that again if I cheated. Well, I figured, "IF" I get caught cheating. I wondered if she would be interested in swinging. To be perfectly honest, I wasn't sure I could pull it off. You had to be really secure with yourself, and I wasn't sure that I was in that place right now. Back to reality, I wanted this week to be over so I headed to the Pittman piece.

The piece consisted of three loops, Sherwood, Dogwood, and Hedgewood. I received a couple of comments/ questions as I did the piece. "Where's Mike? Why are you so late?"

I just answered, "I already did my route. Mike went home early." I repeated that between 12 and 15 times. I finished up and headed to 7-Eleven to get a bottle of water. I was definitely going to become a cooler-carrying guy. Two dollars and change for one bottle of water. I could get a case of twenty-four for five dollars. I spent over twenty-five dollars between the coffee truck and drinks here at 7-Eleven. I was tired and wondered if dehydration was part of the problem. This was a physically demanding job after all. Racking mail, you stand in the same spot for three or four hours. Then you walked for five hours on the clock. Sure, you made up time, but you earned that. I sat and drank my water and watched people go in the store.

Some of the people looked over and I got one, "Yo, mailman." It was Saturday and, for the average Joe, their weekend started yesterday. Mine hadn't started yet. I even had to work tomorrow. At least I didn't have to get up early. I had to be at the office at 10:00 a.m, not bad. I thought of Janet and how lucky I was going to get tonight. Of course, the time flew by when I sat down and took a break. It was always harder to get going again. Newton's laws of motion, A body at rest has a tendency to stay at rest and all that.

I drove back to the office. It was 4:30 and I had until 5:00 to punch out. The Post Office parking lot was packed, I'd never seen it like that before. I parked behind a jeep that was double-parked. I didn't have much, eight empty trays and a handful of outgoing mail. Oh, yeah, two misracked letters. Not bad for a newbie.

As I went up to the dock, I saw the dockmaster Cody. I asked him where to put the outgoing mail. He said, "Right over here, put it in the big bin." When he said big, he meant huge. This thing was four feet by three feet and four feet deep. I could tell from a distance that Cody was drunk. You could practically smell it from four feet away. His eyes were glassy and his words were slurred.

He waved me over, "Come here, come here" he whispered, "how about a drink?" He had a half-pint of something.

I refused, "Thanks, bro, but not today. Definitely next time"

He said, "No problem, that leaves more for the dockmaster."

He looked around and took a swig. As I headed inside, I was surprised how out in the open his drinking was. I went through the swinging doors and there was my boy Yo-yo sitting at the carrier supervisor desk. I could only imagine what Stan would do if he could see how comfortable Eric was in his coveted chair. Maybe one day Eric would be supervisor, after all his ass fit in that chair since day one.

"Yo, Kev, I've been waiting for you. I've been off the clock for an hour. Cummings won't let me get any overtime. Can you believe she thinks I'm malingering with my injury? Does she really think I would rather be cooped up in here instead of out on the road with you guys?" Honestly, I did not know. I felt like maybe he was faking, too. He was telling me one doctor thought it was like Bo Jackson's injury where part of his hip bone was dying. Bo Jackson was a tremendous two-sport athlete who performed at an all-star level in both sports. I couldn't believe his doctor was drawing parallels to Bo. I mean, slipping on bird shit and getting hit in a professional football game was a huge difference.

Now, Regional figureheads were aware of Yo-yo's predicament. Not only did they count how much mail was delivered and kept track of overtime taken by each office, but they also kept statistics on lost work days and injuries. Eric Hartman had been a topic of conversation amongst individuals who didn't really have anything better to do. Since he was injured on his first day, and it was not a clear cut injury, it would actually be easier if he had a broken bone. Ms. Cummings, as Superintendent of postal operations, was taking this bizarre situation personally.

I still had to clear and glanced at the window and saw three carriers waiting. Quentin was first and was talking to Lucy, "Have a great day off. Maybe I'll see you tonight."

"You too, Quentin," Lucy sang.

Syd Weir was up next. He had a registered, delivered, and nine certifieds, six delivered and three left notice. People wonder what's the most secure way to send mail. The answer is registered. Registered was monitored every step of the way. Every time it changed hands, it was signed for. Another indicator is that it costs more to send.

Syd was done. He pointed and said, "Thanks, Lucy. I'm only going tonight so I can see you, so you have to go."

Lucy responded, "I will do my best to make it, but I have lots of school work to do. Otherwise, have a good day off."

I'm up next, "Hey Loose, I had two certified, one delivered and one left notice. Here are the keys. By the way, how was school?" I said as I handed her the key to the mailbox. She smiled as she put the key away in its place.

"It's a lot of work. Some people have dropped out already. I'm keeping up. I have an outline for the paper that is due at the end of the semester, and I'm ahead on my readings. Of course, the key is to be prepared and stay up on the work. I thank God for my mom. She is helping me with my son Julien. So, what are you doing on your day off?" I informed her Stan had me working tomorrow, Sunday.

"Oh, well the express mail slips and the undeliverable express go right here at the window."

Nobody mentioned that information to me, so I responded, "Thanks for letting me know, Lucy. You are an angel"

Lucy looked up at me and smiled, "Bye, Kevin." I wonder if I would give up Janet and her magic if I could have Lucy.

As I went to the locker room to wash up, I saw Syd and remembered that I borrowed his shirt. I let him know, "Hey Syd, your shirt was very lucky for me. I'm going to get it dry cleaned for you."

"You don't have to," as he pointed to his locker.

To which I responded, "Don't have to, want to." I washed up and headed back to route 19. This was my last Saturday on this route since it would be awarded to the highest bidder on Monday and the new "melman" would start next Saturday. I was curious to know what route I'd be delivering. As I left, I took one last glance at the route and was certain that it was not going to look like that on Monday morning.

There were about 12 guys waiting to punch out at 5:00. At 4:59 Quentin punched out. If you remember, he punched in a minute early to start the day. He headed for the door and said, "Let's get out of this dump!" The rest of us waited a moment until 5:00 exactly and then followed suit.

As I headed out the door, Yo-yo ran up to me and asked, "Kev, can I get a ride?" The week was finally over and I was in a good mood, so I said yes. What the heck, in a couple of hours I was going to see my gorgeous girlfriend. As I drove Eric home, he was telling me that Cummings was stressing him out and that Gladys was due at any minute. He told me his other kids could sense something was amiss and were acting up. I was only half listening and, thankfully, the ride went quickly. We arrived at the Hartman home and two kids came running out. They were screaming, "Daddy!" as they ran to him and thankfully not into the street. Gladys looked bigger than she did a couple of days ago. I really didn't see how she could get much bigger.

She looked tired as she waved and yelled, "Thanks, Kev. You're a good friend" *The best,* I thought sarcastically. I drove home and debated picking up a six-pack of beer and then realized that I still had four left in the fridge.

I arrived home and the first thing I did was call Janet. "Hey baby, I was thinking of you all day!"

"Did you just get off work? It's almost 6:00." I explained that I worked two hours overtime and then drove Yo-yo home. I had to explain the Yo-yo nickname. Then I got into the whole Hartman saga. She proceeded to tell me that she and Chrissy will be at the Modern at 9:00.

"9:00?" I repeated. She said Chrissy assured her that they won't go on until 9:30 or 9:45. And Chrissy would not take a chance to miss a minute.

Janet asked me, "Have you ever been to the Modern bar? I don't know why they call it the Modern, it's old and run down.

It's no Bermuda T." We said goodbye and agreed to meet inside around 9:00.

I went upstairs to see my parents. Mom made meatballs and spaghetti. She makes the best meatballs and I gulped them down. Pop said, "Take human bites!" While I was eating, I filled them in on my first week. Mom and Dad were getting an earful of Yo-yo tales, incidents at work, and Janet. When Mom said she hadn't seen much of me, I explained that I racked up eight hours of overtime.

Dad pointed out, "I thought you were part-time?"

"That's in name only. They only have to guarantee me like ten hours a week. Right now, they are shorthanded, eight guys a week are on vacation."

Mom said, "That's a lot. Eat slower, Kevin."

Dad advised, "Grab the overtime when you can. Because when there is none, you can't complain."

I said between bites, "I'm not turning down any overtime, pop. I need the money. I even sort of volunteered to work tomorrow."

Mom questioned, "Tomorrow? On Sunday?"

I informed them, "Yes, I'll be emptying mailboxes and delivering express mail."

Pop responded, "That's my boy."

SATURDAY NIGHT'S ALRIGHT FOR...

I finished my dinner and washed my dish despite mom's objections and knowing she was going to rewash it anyway. I went downstairs and took a 45-minute nap. I woke up at 8:00 and showered. I put on a pair of jeans, black boots, and a black t-shirt that was a little tight. I had worked out in the past and the guns were bigger than most guys. So the t-shirt looked pretty good, although I needed to lay off the brewskis. But not now. Because I was going to drink a beer before I headed to the Modern bar. I turned onto Main Street in Farmingburg, and halfway down the block I saw the Modern. There was a crowd of people in front. I drove around to the back parking lot and it was packed. It was like a huge party going on. There were groups of people hanging out, some drinking and you could smell people smoking weed. The parking lot was crowded and I found a spot towards the back. I went around the front and there was a line to get it. Although there were three other bars on this section of Main Street, the Modern was the only one with a line in front of it. Never dawned on me that there was a cover charge. I wondered if it would help if I mentioned that I worked with Pittman and Yates. I even did a piece on Pittman's route today.

Probably wouldn't get me a discount. So I paid the ten dollars and entered.

Now I knew what Janet meant. The bar was kind of dingy. It packed so I went around to the stage area. This area had little groups of people and space to move. As I maneuvered, I could see Quentin Roosevelt. It was hard to miss a six-foot six white guy with dreads. I headed over there and the Farmingburg Post Office was well represented. There was The Bruce, Steve "Gravy train" Graves, Syd, Benjy Steckel, even Robard was there. He was dressed in jeans and an orange polka dot shirt with a white background, which was quite subdued for him. Then I saw her, my angel, Lucy Consuelo Gonzales-Nieves Martinez Smith. As I walked over, Mick came to me and said, "Hey, J, let me buy you a drink. What will it be?"

As I kept my eye on Lucy, I said to Mick, "Thanks, Mick, a Budweiser will do."

Mick turned to the female bartender with a black tank top and red lipstick, "One club soda and a Budweiser." The bartender winked at Mick. I recalled how MacGregor called Mick an alcoholic. I guess it was true.

Mick handed me the beer and we clinked our drinks, "Here's to you making it through the first week."

It was beyond loud and I noticed how run down this place was. Where do they get the balls to call it the Modern bar? Robard was next to me so I said, "What's up? My name Is Kevin," and I extended my hand.

Very deliberately he said, "I know your name" and didn't shake my hand so I walked away. He was not obligated to shake my hand. So I headed towards Lucy.

"Hey, Lucy, so good to see you."

"Yes, I finished my school work and wanted to support the guys. What a turnout. Have you ever seen them before?"

I said, "No."

Lucy admitted, "It's not my favorite style of music, but I always have so much fun and the crowd goes crazy." I was finished with my beer and asked Lucy if she wanted something. She told me she didn't really drink.

I was about to order and said to the bartender. "Sweetheart…," when I got tapped on the shoulder. I turned around to see Janet and Chrissy. I gave Janet a hug and said, "Hey, babe." She was definitely a little cold towards me and asked, "Who's this?" indicating Lucy.

"Oh, this is Lucy, we work together. Lucy, this is my girlfriend, Janet."

Lucy smiled and extended her hand, "So nice to meet you. Kevin, you are so lucky. She is so pretty."

Janet responded, "Thank you, Lucy. I love your hair."

They kept talking about hair stuff and I turned to Chrissy, "What a turnout."

"Yes, we had to park three parking lots away."

Janet came over and kissed me on the lips, "Your friend is so nice, babe. Can you get me a White Russian and Chrissy a tonic water?"

"Will do" as I turned to the barmaid. I got the drinks and The Bruce, J. Thompkins, said, "I just spoke with 'Where's Your House Key' and he told me they were going on in fifteen minutes. Let's head to the stage. Q, lead the way."

Quentin understood his role, "Oh, yeah, follow me." It was as if the crowd parted and we just followed in the wake of people. We got right up front to the stage.

Lucy turned to me, "You have to love Quentin."

Love? I really liked Q and appreciated his size, but did she have to say love? There was a lot of energy in the bar. I looked over at Janet. She seemed a little bored, I didn't think this was her idea of a good time. So I got really close and hugged her and I gave her a long kiss. When we came up for air, Chrissy smiled at me and rolled her eyes.

Chrissy looked hot. She was wearing black leather pants, a shiny black top, and lots of black eyeliner. She had an awesome body and her outfit was tight. This girl would be hard to turn down. Joey Ramonski came on stage; and of course, he had his ski cap on. He inspected the microphone and taped the set list to the floor in two places. Joey indicated to us two minutes. He walked away and Chrissy asked me, "Are you sure that I will meet Mike Pittman?"

I told her, "Well, there are no guarantees in life, but Mike said he would."

Just then Joey Ramonski came to the microphone, "Here they are straight from their liposuction surgery.....Morbid Obesity" The place exploded. They were doing a really fast upbeat song, a cross between ska and heavy metal. People were jumping up and down and going crazy. Some people were echoing the chorus. Chrissy was going insane and her hair was all over the place. Quentin was pumping his fists, and much smaller guys were jumping into his chest and bouncing off. It was pure pandemonium and it was infectious. People were pushing forward and it was hot. Even Janet seemed to be having a good time. Lucy was smiling ear to ear and admiring the guys on stage. I realized that six days ago I didn't even know Lucy, Janet, or Chrissy. I'd never heard of Morbid Obesity.

The guys played for a good hour. Yates came to the microphone, "We are going to dedicate the last song to our good friends, this group right up front." Yates started laying down some real melodic bass lines, then Pittman came in with some loud heavy guitar riffs. The chorus had lyrics that go, "Insufficient postage, return to sender." Everybody was shaking their fists in the air and jumping all around. Quentin was jumping, too; and I must admit, he was getting some serious altitude. The band must have seriously impressed the music industry guys. They finished and walked off the stage.

Joey Ramonski came to the mic, "Thanks for coming out tonight. We are selling t-shirts and CDs at the door."

The crowd was calling for an encore. The crowd chanted, "More, more."

Joey explained, "Morbid Obesity doesn't do encores; but if

you haven't got your fill, the guys are playing at the Grinch in Bethpage in two weeks. I hope to see you there." You could hear some disappointed fans boo, but the crowd started to thin out.

My first thought was, I want to get Janet out to my car so she can do her thing. Chrissy broke the silence, "When do I get to meet Mike Pittman?"

Quentin said, "Oh, yeah. Let's go see the guys and tell them what a great show. Follow me." We got to the backstage door and there was a guy that was actually bigger than Quentin.

He was talking to a group that was mostly girls when he saw Quentin. "What's up, cuz? " It turned out the guy was actually Quentin's cousin, and Quentin got him the job. Obviously, the job requirements were to be big.

"Q, how many you got?" the big guy asked as they shook hands and shoulder bumped.

Quentin said, "This crew right here," and pointed to us. The big guy looked at us and then smiled as he said, "Hey Lucy, so good to see you."

"Hi Jimmy, the guys were really good tonight."

Jimmy said, "It was a perfect night. The execs were impressed. I'm optimistic. Come on in, everybody. They are still in the back and should be out soon. Help yourself to anything."

We headed in—Lucy, Janet, Chrissy, The Bruce, Syd, and Robard—to the lounge which contained two couches and a bar. I headed over to the bar and asked, "Anybody want anything?" I grabbed a beer. Robard came over, just stood there, and said, "Jack Daniels."

I took a swig and poured Robard a shot and asked Janet, "Hey, babe, anything?"

She replied, "Two waters, one for Chrissy."

The Bruce asked, "Do they have Heineken?" I was doing my intern bartending, rummaging for drinks.

Robard came over as I looked for a Heineken and said, "I would like another Jack Daniels." I gave him the two waters and directed him, "Give these to those two hot girls over there on that couch." I found a Heineken and called, "Bruce J., here."

I gave the bottle of Jack Daniels to Robard, "Help yourself, bro." I finished my beer and realized how thirsty I was. I grabbed another beer when the office door opened. Three guys, one older guy, and two in their twenties came out.

One said, "Hello" and they left by Jimmie's door. Joey Ramonski stuck his head out of the office door and then ducked back inside. We heard jubilant shouting from inside the office. The Bruce was trying to wrestle the Jack Daniels bottle from Robard. Robard was chugging the whiskey and he had put a good dent in it.

The office door opened and Pittman, Yates, Joey Ramonski, and the drummer came out. Lucy started clapping and Chrissy was yelling and clapping.

Joey said, "These guys are going places."

Pittman replied, "Now, now, let's relax and not jump to conclusions. It was only a verbal agreement. We need to make it legal, you know, lawyers and all. But damn, yes, they made some awesome promises."

Yates said, "Tonight was the turning point. Let's make a toast!"

Joey said, "I gotta go and help Wojo with the merch, see ya."

Lucy went up to Pittman and said, "I'm going home, I'm really tired. Goodbye, everybody." As she slipped out the door, Yates was raising a glass with everybody else, "Morbid Obesity. To infinity and beyond!"

Somebody yelled out, "Hear, hear." Yates was holding court with a crowd and Pittman was sitting on one of the couches. He was sweaty and tired.

This affair was way past everyone's bedtime. Well, everyone that worked in the Post Office. I grabbed Chrissy by the hand. This was our opportunity. We headed over to Pittman. He saw us approaching so he stood up like a gentleman. "Hey, J, I'm glad you came. What did you think?"

"After that display, I'm a fan. I had a really good time."

He asked, "Is this your friend?"

Chrissy looked a little like what could best be described as star struck. "Yes, this is my friend Chrissy, and right here is my girlfriend, Janet." I grabbed Janet by the hand and pulled her over.

Chrissy gushed, "I love you guys. Can I ask you a question? After the song 'Are you talking to me,' you did a song that I'm not familiar with."

"You are truly a fan. That's a new song that we're still working on. This was the first time we performed it. I'm so impressed. That deserves a free t-shirt."

"Yes, I would love a t-shirt. Can I have the one that you're wearing?"

"It's all sweaty. We have some nice women's tank tops."

"Nope, I want that one, please."

"Okay, let me get a dry shirt anyway. 'Where's Your House Key!'"

Wojo came in, "Hey, guys, we had our best night merch wise." It was getting late, especially for postal workers. Jimmy was letting in other well-wishers and hangers-on and it was getting loud and crowded. I felt a little out of place.

Janet kissed me and looked me in the eyes, "That was so nice, what you did for Chrissy."

I blurted out, "Baby, your friends are my friends," and I kissed her again. I was thinking, *You can show your appreciation later.*

Janet informed me, "Chrissy is going to stay. Let's go to your place and you can drive me home later."

"Sounds like a plan." I realized that while I was happy for the guys, we did everything we needed to do here. I went over to Yates to say goodbye. Pittmann was over in the corner, surrounded, Chrissy wasn't far away. Robard was right next to her and it seemed she was ignoring him. Janet had already said goodbye to her, so we left.

We made out a little in my car. Janet opened my belt and said, "Drive." I did as I was told and pulled out of the parking lot, while she stroked little Johnson. I know—how appropriate, my last name and my unit. As I turned off Main Street and onto Farmingburg Turnpike, Janet bent over and did her thing. She was licking and sucking as I drove. She stopped for a second and asked, "Can you handle it? I don't want to die." I told her to continue, that I didn't want to die either, but it would be an awesome way to check out. I tell you, this girl was awesome at giving head. I was curious to know why. Obviously, she'd had lots of practice. I was going to ask her if she watches porn. Well, I should ask if she studies it.

I had to stop the car as there was a red light and boom went the dynamite. I exploded in her mouth and she was still going until it was too much for me. "Stop, stop, that's good," I said as she sat up and spit out the window. We were still stopped even though the light was green. A car went by and honked. The horn brought me back to reality, and I started to drive again. I don't know why but I mumbled, "Thanks."

Janet informed me, "I like to make my guy happy. When we get to your place, we are going to shower and it will be your turn to reciprocate. You're going downtown, buddy boy."

"Good. I'll show you one of my talents." I turned to her and showed her that I can touch my nose with my tongue.

"Oh, baby, you have potential!" she said as we both laughed.

I made small talk. "The morbid ones had a great night. Seems they got a good response from the music execs."

Janet said, "They seem like really good guys, too."

Before I knew it, we were pulling up to my folks' house. I parked in the driveway and the lights were off in the house. We went around the back and down the stairs to my spot. We went in and I offered Janet a drink. She wanted water. She told me to go first in the shower; it was a small shower stall. I took my shower and it felt great. When I came out, Janet was naked and wearing my slippers. "This is a pretty good place you have," she observed.

"Well, it will do for now. When I save up some money and you are licensed, maybe you can find a house for us." She kissed me as she took the clean towel I handed her. I dried off and got in bed to wait for her.

SUNDAY. THEY HAVE MAIL ON SUNDAYS?

I opened my eyes and looked at the clock. It was 7:00 a.m. I fell asleep. Janet was still here and she looked great, partly because she was naked; but she looked good even without make-up on. She was a natural beauty. I tried not to wake her as I got up to pee, which was hard because I was rigid. I accomplished the feat and brushed my teeth which I didn't do before I fell asleep.

I got back to the bed and she was semi-awake, "Hey, sleepyhead, I hope you don't mind that I stayed over." She laughed as she said, "You were out like a rock. I tried to wake you up, I even kissed little Johnson, nothing" Janet was sitting up and the sheets were around her waist and her perky tits were jiggling as she laughed.

Suddenly, little Johnson wasn't so little anymore. I was proud of him as he stood at attention. Janet moved the sheet away and I laid down next to her. We kissed and she said, "I'm so wet and horny, fuck me."

Now, I didn't need to be told twice, but I was sensible, "What about protection?"

"I just finished my period, FUCK ME!" So I obliged. I have to admit, the girl was beyond wet. She was slippery. We had good chemistry and we fucked like animals. It seemed she had multiple orgasms, at least she said she did. I rolled off her when I came and we hugged each other. "Good job," she said. We kissed a little more as we laid on our sides and we fell asleep in each other's arms. I opened my eyes and the first thing I saw was Janet's face. I thought to myself that I was one lucky bastard.

I glanced at the clock and it was 10:40. 10:40? Shit, I was supposed to be at the Post Office at 10:00. I jumped up out of bed, and Janet woke up. "What are you doing? Where are you going?"

I informed her, "I gotta go to work. I was supposed to be there at 10:00."

"Baby, it's Sunday."

I explained, "I have to empty mailboxes and deliver express mail."

She replied, "I think you mentioned something about that."

"Get dressed. I'll drive you home." Janet looked at me mischievously, "You are already late. You need to calm down. Let's go another round."

I was a typical guy so my response was just, "Okay." We kissed and she turned around and I slid little Johnson right in. I wanted to come real fast, but knowing I was late for work prolonged the act. This girl liked to fuck, and I liked to fuck her. She was moaning kinda loud and I was concerned about mom and dad hearing her. Again, this prolonged me finishing. I started smacking her ass and boom went the dynamite. We were both out of breath.

Janet gushed, "Wow, babe, we are good together. Get dressed. I'll get Chrissy to come pick me up. I'm going to sleep a little more. I just need the address here."

I said, "Or you can stay and we can do this again. We can go somewhere for dinner."

"We will see," she said as she rolled over and closed her eyes. I got dressed, brushed my teeth, and combed my hair. I headed out the door as quietly as I could. I got in my car and headed out of the driveway. I arrived at Farmingburg Post Office at 11:45.

I figured if I didn't punch in or out, Stan wouldn't know that I was late. I got the jeep keys and the mailbox keys. I found the list of mailboxes I had to hit. I put about 15 of those empty white mail bins in the jeep and drove to the first mailbox to empty it. It was about a third full as I exchanged an empty bin. It didn't take long to finish the residential area boxes. Some boxes were practically empty. Now it was on to the business side. These boxes had much more mail. A couple of the mailboxes were more than a bin. Letters fell out of the mailboxes that were really full. The last box that I had to empty was at the college. I drove over and the campus was for the most part empty.

Now I had to go to the mail processing center at Melville to drop off the outgoing mail and to pick up the express mail. It was not a long drive and I pulled in the Melville parking lot. The parking lot was huge, but only a tenth full right now. Here in Melville they received and distributed tons of mail every day. Tractor-trailers brought in mail and, somehow, they sorted it and sent the mail to the respective Post Offices. There was a loading dock where at least twelve tractor-trailers could fit. I backed up and noticed there was a guy sitting there smoking a cigarette.

I asked him, "Hey, bro, it's my first time doing this. Do I leave the outgoing here?"

He slowly walked over, "Yes, put the mail bins up here. You're from Farmingburg, you're late. You're the last office to pick up the express. Did you know that express mail is supposed to be delivered by 12:00 noon?"

I lied, "I had car trouble, had to wait for my girlfriend to drive me to work."

"I don't care, I'm just saying" he gave me a big orange and blue nylon bag. "Expresses are in the bag. You might want to put 11:59 as the time delivered. Good luck." I told him thanks and drove away. As I was driving through this huge parking lot, I realized that I had to open the bag to know where I had to go. So I stopped and inspected the contents of the bag. Six express mail, five envelopes, and one box. Four business and two residential.

The business section was closer so I decided to start there. Wow, one express mail was for Four Seasons. I arranged the mail for the closest one. First up was an appliance store and I made the delivery. I put down the time of delivery as 11:59. The guy signing didn't notice or care and just signed. The next closest was Four Seasons. I drove by and it was definitely closed.

Next was for a small machine shop on Pittman's route, route 44. There was a car outside the building so I rang the bell. I waited and rang again. I was about to leave when a guy came to the door. I can smell he'd been smoking weed. Personally, I smoke a little myself. I loved the smell of marijuana. I breathed deeply when someone was smoking. Of course, it wouldn't get me high. I just loved the smell. I mentioned, "Ah, the good stuff."

The guy asked me, "You want to smoke?" I told him thanks, but not while I was working. The box was the size of a shoebox. The guy seemed happy that the box came. I noticed that the box originated in Arizona and was addressed to Wayne Brady. I put down the time again as 11:59. I instructed, "I need you to sign here, Wayne."

Wayne responded, "Huh? Oh no that's my partner," as he signed. He said, "Thanks. Are you sure you don't want to puff a little bit?" I said maybe next time and got in the jeep. I headed to the last business and it was closed. So now to the residential. At the first one, nobody answered and I left notice. The second was in the apartments on Mick's route. I parked in the parking lot and had to go to the third floor. The guy was home and seemed surprised that we delivered on Sunday. I went down in the elevator to my jeep and noticed a familiar figure looking into the jeep. It was Beauregard, so I said, "Hey, Beauregard, whatcha doing?"

"Oh, hey I was wondering if I got any mail."

"There's no mail today, just express mail," I said to him.

I was finished for the day. I hoped Janet was still at my place and maybe we would do it again. I drove down Main Street and noticed the Portsmiths sitting outside. Mrs. Portsmith looked over and waved. I waved back as Mr. Portsmith looked over. Although I couldn't hear him, I was sure he was complaining about something.

I drove into the Post Office parking lot. It was only 1:20 and I actually had half a day to myself. I put the non-delivered express mail and delivered receipts at the accountable window. I walked past good old route 19 and was proud of myself that it was all cleaned up. I was certain that it was not going to look like that tomorrow morning. On the way home, I bought a six-pack as my plans were to do my laundry, drink beer, and watch baseball. Doing laundry was easy when you could do it at home, and you felt like you performed a major accomplishment. You sort it, put in a load, and half an hour later move it to the dryer, put more in the washer, and so on. Then, when people asked what you accomplished today, you can say laundry and be proud of yourself. I really wanted to wash my sheets, you might be able to figure out why. I pulled in the driveway and headed towards the backyard. My mom was gardening. I said hello and bent down and gave her a kiss.

She asked, "Whatcha doing, sweetie?"

I informed her that I was at work. Mom was surprised, like most people, that mail carriers worked on Sunday. "I guess it makes sense that they deliver overnight mail on Sunday. If they mail it on Saturday, overnight is Sunday." Mom saw me glance at my door and said, "Your friend left about an hour ago. If you don't mind me asking…"

I jumped in and told her how I met Janet while delivering mail. "She's a receptionist and is studying to be a real estate agent, in hopes of starting a practice with her cousin. She's a nice girl."

Mom commented, "Well, you only met her this week and she spent the night. You two made quite a ruckus this morning. I don't appreciate that." I was thinking, *We made a ruckus twice.*

Mom attended church every week, so she had conservative views on certain topics.

I quickly changed the subject, "What's for dinner?"

She let me know it was roast beef and it would be ready at 5:00. I said, "Alright mom, I have laundry to do. I work Monday through Saturday next week. I'm going to be working lots of overtime. I'll see you for dinner."

Mom was concerned, "That's why we don't see much of you. Don't overdo it, sweetie."

"It is what it is, mom." I went downstairs and started a load of laundry. I laid down on the bed. Maybe I won't wash the sheets, they smelled like Janet. I gave my baby a call.

She answered the phone and I asked her, "So, babe, what did you do all day besides think of me?"

She laughed, "I did think about you a lot. I like you, Kevin."

I was glad to hear that because I had feelings for her. "You were also on my mind quite often today, baby."

We chit chatted for a while and decided before hanging up that I would call her that night. I threw my clothes in the dryer and started my whites. I put on the baseball game and cracked open a beer. The game had already started, and it didn't look good for the home team. Chooch must have bet on them. I thought that in only seven days, this job had consumed most of my time and infiltrated my mind. My dad knocked on the door to let me know that dinner was ready. He brought up the noise that Janet and I made earlier that day. He suggested we turn on the radio or TV extra loud next time. He then winked at me and said, "Way to go, son." I followed pop up the stairs and had dinner with the folks. I regaled them with my tales of the past week. We laughed and they seemed really interested in Emma, the red menace, and Beauregard. They even asked some questions about them. We had a good time. I got up to do the dishes and got in a small argument with my mom about it. One day she should surprise me and let me do the dishes. I went downstairs and my laundry was done, so I folded my whites.

The end of the Mets game was on; and while they made a valiant comeback, they still lost. I knew that I was not going to have much time during the week so I did a little dusting and then vacuumed. I watched *60 Minutes;* and when it was over, I called Janet. I had to admit I was somewhat smitten with her. What wasn't to like? She was fun to be with, she had realistic goals, she was confident, and of course, there was the obvious, amazing sex. I was aware that with this crazy work schedule, I needed her. Our relationship was an outlet for the stress, and I loved the attention she gave to me. I looked at the clock. It was only 9:30; but if I wanted eight hours of shut-eye, I had better get to bed. I got ready and put my head down on the pillow. In less than two minutes I was asleep.

168 HOURS = ONE WEEK

I woke up, got dressed, and ate a bowl of cereal. I drove to work and, as it so happened, I parked in the same exact spot as last week. One week ago, one hundred and sixty-eight hours ago, I pulled into this very parking spot, not knowing what lay in store for me. I recalled how scared, apprehensive, and uncertain I felt last Monday. Well, I was certain about one thing. I was certain that I had worn the wrong shoes. Remember those shoes? OMG, what was I thinking? At least no one called me "Shoes" anymore. I sit here today and I feel like a seasoned veteran. Again, being a letter carrier was not skilled labor. You racked the mail and you delivered the mail, not much to it. There wasn't a great deal of room for improvement, perhaps a little, but that's it. I guess the key was to not let the job drive you crazy. As I walked to the office to embark on my second week, I wondered what was going to happen next. What was in store in my future in the Post Office...

ABOUT THE AUTHOR

Kevin Johnson is an Army veteran and retired Adjunct professor. In a previous life Kevin was a letter carrier for eight years on Long Island. He wishes to share some of his insights and stories of his time in the wool pant army. Let's face it someone had to write a book about it.

www.ingramcontent.com/pod-product-compliance
Lightning Source LLC
Chambersburg PA
CBHW072011070526
44583CB00015B/1433